Jean Nicolas Grou, Alexander Clinton, Samuel Hanna Frisbee

The characteristics of true devotion

Jean Nicolas Grou, Alexander Clinton, Samuel Hanna Frisbee

The characteristics of true devotion

ISBN/EAN: 9783743383524

Manufactured in Europe, USA, Canada, Australia, Japa

Cover: Foto ©Lupo / pixelio.de

Manufactured and distributed by brebook publishing software (www.brebook.com)

Jean Nicolas Grou, Alexander Clinton, Samuel Hanna Frisbee

The characteristics of true devotion

THE COMPLETE ASCETIC WORKS

OF THE

Rev. J. N. GROU,
Of the Society of Jesus.

TRANSLATED FROM THE FRENCH.

EDITED BY

Rev. SAMUEL H. FRISBEE, S.J.

THE CHARACTERISTICS

OF

TRUE DEVOTION.

THE CHARACTERISTICS OF TRUE DEVOTION.

TRANSLATED FROM THE FRENCH OF
THE REV. J. N. GROU,
Of the Society of Jesus,

BY THE REV. ALEXANDER CLINTON, S.J.

A NEW EDITION.

REVISED AND EDITED AFTER COMPARISON WITH ALL EXISTING EDITIONS IN FRENCH AND ENGLISH BY

REV. SAMUEL H. FRISBEE, S.J.,
Spiritual Director of Woodstock College.

NEW YORK, CINCINNATI, CHICAGO:
BENZIGER BROTHERS,
Printers to the Holy Apostolic See.

1895.

GULIELMUS PARDOW

Praepositus Provinciae Marylandiae Neo-Eboracensis Soc. Jesu.

Quum librum cui titulus " Characteristics of True Devotion " a J. N. Grou nostrae Societatis conscriptum, et a S. H. Frisbee, ejusdem Societatis sacerdote recensitum, aliqui ejusdem Societatis revisores, quibus id commissum fuit, recognoverint et in lucem edi posse probaverint ; facultatem concedimus ut typis mandetur, si ita iis ad quos pertinet videbitur.

In cujus rei fidem has litteras manu nostra subscriptas, et sigillo officii munitas dedimus.

WOODSTOCK COLLEGE,

die Sept. 28, 1894.

GULIELMUS PARDOW, S.J.

Praepositus Provinciae Neo-Eboracensis.

Imprimatur.

✠ MICHAEL AUGUSTINE,

Archbishop of New York.

NEW YORK, *October* 1, 1894.

NOV 3 1958

Copyright, 1894, by Benziger Brothers.

CONTENTS.

	PAGE
A WORD TO THE READER	9
A SHORT SKETCH OF THE AUTHOR AND HIS WORKS	15

CHAPTER

I. Introductory; the Object of this Book.	19
II. True Devotion defined	23
III. What we owe to God; the Motives for Devotedness	27
IV. That every other Devotedness should be subordinate to that which we owe to God	31
V. That the First Object of our Devotedness should be the Glory of God and the Accomplishment of his Will	33
VI. That the Second Object of Man's Devotion should be his own Sanctification. The Reasons why he should seek it	36
VII. The Third Object of our Devotion, our Happiness	39

CHAPTER	PAGE
VIII. Qualities of True Devotedness to God. The Spirit of Prayer	43
IX. That Devotion to be True must be Interior	47
X. That Devotion should appear in our External Actions. Reasons which prove this	53
XI. The Error of those who exclude Mental Prayer from Devotion..	57
XII. That it is an Abuse to Multiply too much the Practices of Devotion	63
XIII. That we must give ourselves up to God without Restriction and without Reserve	66
XIV. That True Devotion admits of no Division	72
XV. That Devotion is for Persons of every Age	81
XVI. That Devotion extends to all Conditions of Life	87
XVII. That Love is the only Foundation of Devotion	93
XVIII. That to be Truly Devoted we must forget our own Interests and seek God only	97

CHAPTER		PAGE
XIX.	The Fatal Effects of Self-love on Devotion	101
XX.	That Devotion gives Birth to Confidence. The Good Effects and the Necessity of this Confidence	105
XXI.	That Devotion begets Self-knowledge and consequently Humility	110
XXII.	Simplicity and the Fear of being noticed are the Characteristics of True Devotion. How few possess them	114
XXIII.	Mortification of the Senses is another Quality of Devotion	121
XXIV.	That Mortification of the Will is Essential to Devotion	125
XXV.	Various Qualities of Devotion	131
XXVI.	Some other Qualities of Devotion	135
XXVII.	That Devotion Perfects and Corrects the Character	140
XXVIII.	That Devotion, far from contracting the Mind, aids its Development	144
XXIX.	That Devotion elevates the Heart of Man above all that is not God.	152

CHAPTER		PAGE
XXX.	The Man Truly Devout regards everything in Relation to Eternity and to the Will of God	158
XXXI.	Conduct of the Truly Devout Man in regard to his Neighbor.	163
XXXII.	The Difference between the Politeness of the World and the Cordiality of True Devotion	171
XXXIII.	The Truly Devout Man possesses all Civil Qualities	177
XXXIV.	The Truly Devout Man possesses the only true Happiness that can be enjoyed on Earth	180
XXXV.	That Jesus Christ is the Grand Model of Perfect Devotedness.	185
XXXVI.	Three Efficacious Means to acquire True Devotion.	190
XXXVII.	Reflections on the Characteristics of True Devotion.	196

A WORD TO THE READER.

THIS little book has been the most widely circulated of all Father Grou's writings. Forty editions in French, and, including the present version, four translations into English, show that it, indeed, has been well known; yet to-day there is no reliable edition in print, so that some of those who take it up will meet with it for the first time. A few words about it and its author may not, therefore, be amiss. It was published for the first time at Paris in 1788, and is the second in order of time of Father Grou's ascetic writings, being preceded in 1786 by *Morale tirée des Confessions de Saint Augustin.* It was translated into English by Father Alexander Clinton, S.J., who was chaplain at Lullworth Castle, where Father Grou spent the last years of his life in exile, and was published at London, in 1791, under the title "The Characters of Real Devotion." A second edition was issued at Dublin in 1795, a third in 1801, and a fourth in 1838. An entirely new translation was published at Baltimore in 1832 by Fielding Lucas, Jr., entitled "Portraiture of True Devotion." By whom this translation was made we have been unable to ascertain. A third translation into English was published by Thomas Whittaker, New York, 1882. The preface is signed by Ellen M. Fogg, who, we presume, is the translator.

Of these different versions the one by Father Clinton is by far the most reliable. Though the English is antiquated and the version at times too literal, he evidently understood French well and has caught the meaning and the spirit of the author. The same cannot be said of the other two translations. "The Portraiture of True Devotion" does not aim at a literal rendering of the French, and manifests throughout a lack of simplicity and a search after long words and an exuberant style, entirely unsuited to the character of the work. The translation published by Whittaker is in better style, but there are many phrases which show that the translator did not understand well the French idiom. There are also some omissions, in one case of a whole chapter, which we are told in the preface that the translator "has taken the liberty to omit since they seemed only adapted to the religious, and in no way to the secular." Though this edition was gotten out for the members of the Anglican Church, it does not bear explicit evidence of "being adapted so as to bring it into harmony with the Book of Common Prayer and Anglican Divinity," yet it contains expressions which no Catholic would use, and which Father Grou would certainly never have approved. More frequent, however, are the errors arising from a misunderstanding of the language in which Father Grou wrote. For these reasons this translation cannot be recommended.

The editor of the present edition has taken Father Clinton's version as a basis, and has compared it diligently with the revised French edition of Father Cadrès and with the other two English versions. In correcting the translation of Father Clinton, his aim has been to give in modern English just what Father Grou wrote, preferring a literal rendering, even sometimes at the sacrifice of smoothness, to an equivalent paraphrase. In regard to the title of the book, "The Characteristics of True Devotion" has been chosen rather than Father Clinton's "The Characters of Real Devotion," as the use of the word "Characters" in the sense employed is to-day unusual. Since Father Grou uses the word "devotion" in the sense of devotedness, "The Characteristics of True Devotedness" would be a more exact title; but as the work is already known by the name of "True Devotion," and as Father Grou explains at the beginning of Chapter II. that all true devotion means a devotedness or a consecration, it has been judged better to keep the name "The Characteristics of True Devotion."

As to the matter of which the book treats and its importance, the judgment of the censor appointed to examine the first edition leaves nothing to be added. It is prefixed to the best French editions, and we add it here in English for the benefit of our readers. "This excellent book reveals in its pious author a profound knowledge of the inner life of those souls which are working earnestly at their sanctification. He explains, first, what is to be understood by the word "devotion," then he gives the motives for practising it, points out its real object, and indicates the means of acquiring it. From all these characteristics, which constitute a faithful portrait of devotion, those who make it their aim to lead a pious life, even though in the world, can draw the greatest profit for their advancement in Christian perfection. Those, on the contrary, who make their whole life of devotion to consist in delusive practices, will find here infallible rules to reform their ideas and to undeceive them in regard to what, under the appearance of piety, is only hypocrisy, and to instruct them in a true devotion, which has for its foundation the most complete devotedness of the heart to all which can procure the glory of God, the edification of the neighbor, and their own sanctification."

WOODSTOCK COLLEGE,
WOODSTOCK, MARYLAND,
October, 1894.

A SHORT SKETCH OF THE AUTHOR AND HIS WORKS.*

JEAN NICOLAS GROU was born at Calais on the 23d of November, 1751, and at the age of fifteen he entered the Society of Jesus. According to all accounts, he made his first studies in the college of Louis-Le-Grand, at that time under the direction of the Jesuits. He had scarcely finished his course of teaching and his theological studies, when an excellent translation of Plato gave him a distinguished rank among the writers of that epoch. The decree suppressing the So-

* For fuller details, both of the life of Father Grou and his Works, see the Sketch of his Life and Works at the beginning of Vol. 1 of "The Interior of Jesus and Mary." This Short Sketch is only added for those who may not have that work.

ciety in France obliged him to seek refuge in Lorraine, where he made his last vows, at Pont-à-Mousson, in 1765 or 1766. Later on, a change of circumstances led him to Holland and gave him leisure to continue his labors on Greek philosophy.

Some years after, having returned to Paris at the invitation of the Archbishop, he was charged with the direction of a religious Community. In 1792 Providence offered him a secure refuge in England from the persecutions of the French Revolution. He was received into the family of Mr. Weld at Lullworth Castle, dear to American Catholics as being the place where our first bishop, the Right Reverend John Carroll, was consecrated Bishop of Baltimore. Here his merits and his well-tried virtue won him the veneration and the esteem of all who had the advantage of knowing him.

He died in 1803, at Lullworth Castle, where the Weld family had so nobly and generously offered him hospitality—a hospitality which he richly repaid by his excellent counsels, and by writing for Mr. Weld and his children some of his most valuable ascetic works.

During the last years preceding his departure from France, Father Grou, obliged to keep in seclusion on account of the Revolution, spent much time in writing on pious subjects. It is to this pronounced taste for retirement and labor that we are indebted for several excellent works that he published before leaving Paris. There appeared successively in the space of six or seven years: "Moral Instructions Extracted from the Confessions of St. Augustin," "Characteristics of True Devotion," "Spiritual Maxims, with Explanations," "The Science of the Crucifix," and "The Practical Science of the Crucifix." These were followed, when he had taken refuge in England, by "Meditations on the Love of God," "The Christian Sanctified by the Lord's Prayer," "The Interior of Jesus and Mary," "The Gift of One's Self to God," "The School of Jesus Christ." All these works, inspired by an ardent zeal for the greater glory of God and the salvation of souls, have already borne abundant fruit, and may be read with great profit by every Christian desirous of perfection. Several of these works have been at various times translated into English, but are now out of print; others have never been translated. That so valuable works may be rendered available for all who read English, the editor, supported by the publishers, is engaged in bringing out a complete edition in English of all the works mentioned above. "The Interior of Jesus and Mary" has already appeared; "The Characteristics of True Devotion" is the second of the series. The others will follow, three being already translated and awaiting revision.

THE CHARACTERISTICS
OF
TRUE DEVOTION.

CHAPTER I.

INTRODUCTORY. OBJECT OF THIS BOOK.

NOTWITHSTANDING the general decay of piety, there are many who still profess devotion. Few, however, have a just idea of it, almost all following in its regard their prejudices, their imagination, their inclination, or their self-love. Hence arises that infinite number of defects to which the devout of both sexes, of every age, rank, and condition, are subject, and which are wrongfully ascribed to devotion itself. These defects are not always hurtful to salvation, but they hinder perfection and are obstacles to holiness. To the worldly they are an occasion of raillery and of blasphemy; to the weak, a subject of scandal; to ordinary Christians, a pretext which keeps them in their state of tepidity and deters them from embracing the devout life. What powerful reasons these are to induce pious souls, zealous for the glory of God and for their own and their neighbors' interests, to conceive in the sense of the Gospel an exact notion of devotion, and then to express it in their conduct!

In this little book I purpose to set before my readers a faithful picture of devotion. I invite them to observe all its features with an attentive eye, and then to cast a look on themselves. Self love is so blind, the human will is so weak, that I dare not hope that they will draw from this comparative view all the advantage which naturally might be expected. For people in general do not see themselves as they really are, or a long habit, become almost a second nature, takes from many the courage and even the desire of becoming better, while others find the model to be too perfect, and, in the despair of attaining to it, do not even try to approach it.

Be that as it may, I shall think myself happy if a few reap benefit from this book. Besides, I do not write for devout people only. Many Christians hesitate between an ordinary life and an open profession of solid piety. This work is perhaps the means which God chooses to make use of to determine them, and to fix them unalterably in virtue. Sinners daily return to God. They have hitherto been ignorant of the manner of serving him; they will be glad to find a little book to instruct them, the reading of which will require but a few hours. Finally, young people who begin to give themselves to God need to be enlightened and taught the right road that leads to him. As they have no prejudices to fight against, no bad habits to correct, it will suffice to point out to them the path, to engage them to walk in it, and thus preserve themselves from the errors and imperfections of a devotion misunderstood.

To our youth in particular, then, do I recommend this book. Those who are charged with their education may put it into their hands when they judge them fit to understand and profit by it; that is, at the age in which their minds and their hearts are sufficiently expanded. I do not think it advisable for them to read it sooner. The first impression is always the most decisive for the good or bad effect of a work of piety; if once it fails, its credit will hardly ever be established. It is, therefore, better to wait until this impression can be solid and well-grounded.

CHAPTER II.

TRUE DEVOTION DEFINED.

WHAT is devotion? Each one defines it in his own way. To a worldling, devotion consists in believing in God and in holding some principles of religion. To a saint, it consists in being absorbed and lost in God. Between these two extremes there is almost an endless number of definitions, which are more or less exact as they approach one or recede from the other.

To define it exactly, I adhere to the word itself and to the idea which it expresses. The word "devotion" comes from the Latin, and in our language it precisely signifies the state of being devoted or a consecration. Therefore, to be devout is the same thing as to be devoted or consecrated to God. It is upon the idea which the term of "being devoted" offers to the mind that I shall ground whatever I have to say on devotion, after having premised that, when God and our duties towards him are in question, the word should be taken in its most serious and broadest sense.

Now, in English as well as in Latin, we know no expression that is stronger than that of "being devoted," in order to express intimate attachment, absolute and voluntary dependence, affectionate zeal,— in a word, a disposition of the mind and heart of wholly submitting one's self to the will of another, of anticipating his wishes, of embracing his interests, and of sacrificing everything for his sake. Thus we say of a child, a servant, a subject, that he is devoted to his father, to his master, to his prince. We also say that a man is devoted to ambition, or to any other passion, when he only thinks of satisfying it; when he seeks every means, directs all his views and enterprises to that purpose, and when it so absorbs him that he hardly can pay attention to any other object.

The being devoted to God comprises all this in the very highest degree; and it adds, besides, a consecration, in virtue of which he who is consecrated belongs no longer to himself,—has no longer a right over himself; but belongs by an act of religion, the most sacred and the most irrevocable, to the Supreme Being to whom he has devoted himself.

Such is the idea which I form to myself of devotion, by explaining the word according to its precise signification. The practice of it, I own, has its beginning, its progress, and its perfection; but the act of consecration should be full, entire, and perfect in the will at the very moment in which it is formed. Without going further, and from this simple definition, we may already judge how rare devotion is among Christians, and whether we ourselves be devout.

CHAPTER III.

WHAT WE OWE GOD; THE MOTIVES FOR DEVOTEDNESS.

THE devotedness which we owe to God is singular in its kind; it is founded on titles which appertain to him alone, and which he cannot share with any one else. God is our first beginning and our last end. He has created us, and he preserves us every moment. We are indebted to him for all the advantages we possess both of soul and body: the heavens, the earth, and all the good things we enjoy are the work of his hands and the gifts of his liberal beneficence. He disposes at pleasure of every event, and his providence has only our welfare in view in all its designs and arrangements.

He has made us to know him, to love

him, to serve him, and thereby to merit to possess him through all eternity. Enriched, from our very origin, with all the benefits of nature and of grace, a never-ending happiness was attached to the observance of a precept, the most simple, the most just, and the most easy. But having fallen from that supernatural state through the disobedience of our first parents, God has reinstated us in it by an admirable invention of his love: giving us his own Son, and taking vengeance on him for our sins, that he might have only mercy for us.

To the general benefit of redemption, add those blessings which are particular—birth in the bosom of the Catholic Church, the true religion, a good education, so many graces of preservation, so many sins forgiven, the tender reproaches and secret invitations to return to him, the many marks, in short, of a special love.

God is our sovereign good, and, to speak

justly, he is our only good. As we have received all from him, so also do we expect all from him in future, as we can be happy only through him. He is our King, our Lawgiver, our Rewarder, the Supreme Arbiter of our destiny. Add to this what he is in himself, the eternity and the infinity of his being and of his perfections. Crown all this with what he is to us in the person of Jesus Christ.

Pause now for a moment; reflect on each one of these titles, which I have barely mentioned; weigh the force of each; estimate its full value; appreciate the claims it has upon you, the sentiments it demands from you, and the obligations it imposes upon you. After having considered each separately, reunite them, and conceive, if you can, the immense extent of the duties which they entail upon you. Measure the capacity of your heart; see if it could discharge the debts which it owes to God, although it were to exhaust itself in respect, love, gratitude, and submission; judge whether your devotedness, how far soever you may carry it, will ever bear any proportion to so many claims upon it.

CHAPTER IV.

THAT EVERY OTHER DEVOTEDNESS SHOULD BE SUBORDINATE TO THAT WHICH WE OWE TO GOD.

THAT every other act of devotedness, even the most lawful, cannot enter into comparison with this is most evident. But besides, every act of devotedness that should stand in opposition to it, that should in the least trench upon it, or even that were not entirely subordinate to it, would be an outrage which God necessarily must condemn and punish. The homage, the respect, the love, the obedience, which we pay to any creature whatever, are no farther just and pleasing to God than he himself commands and authorizes them; no farther than when they keep within the bounds which he has prescribed; no farther than when they are referred to him, and are the expression of the supreme homage, of the infinite respect, of the unparalleled love, and of the absolute obedience which are due to him alone. The true Christian knows but one devotedness, of which all the others are only an extension and an application, namely, that which is due to God. He consecrates to him alone his mind, his heart, and his body; for him alone does he breathe, think, and act; God is the principle, the motive, and the end of all the duties he fulfils towards his fellow-beings.

CHAPTER V.

THAT THE FIRST OBJECT OF OUR DEVOTION SHOULD BE THE GLORY OF GOD AND THE ACCOMPLISHMENT OF HIS WILL.

THE first and grand object of devotion or devotedness (for I shall make use of these two terms indifferently) is, then, the glory of God and the accomplishment of his will. God himself, in all his works, can have no other motive, and he does not allow a Christian to do so; rather, he absolutely forbids him to substitute any other. We exist only to glorify God, and we can glorify him only by loving and obeying him. This glory of God must hold the first place in our thoughts and in our desires; it must be the spring of all our actions. Every other intention, however good, however holy, should have in our hearts only the second place.

This it is which our Lord teaches in the prayer he has given us. The first petitions relate only to God and to the interests of his glory. *Our Father, who art in heaven, hallowed be thy name:* let all rational creatures praise thee, adore thee, and emulously celebrate thy holiness; let them imitate thee, in becoming holy themselves because thou art holy, and perfect as thou art perfect; and be thou hallowed in them and by them. *Thy kingdom come:* may all creatures acknowledge thee for their only Sovereign; may they establish thee the absolute Master of their hearts, and may they invite thee to exercise over them that supreme dominion of which thou art so jealous! *Thy will be done on earth as it is in heaven.* The angels and the blessed know no other law than thy will; it is the principle of the order, of the peace, and of the charity which reigns amongst them, and they place all their happiness in accomplishing it. May it be the same here below among men; may they use their liberty solely in submitting it, not only to thy orders, but also to thy good pleasure, and to the appointments of thy adorable providence! Such ought to be the most intimate and the most ardent aspirations of true devotion. Are they ours? Does the heart accompany the lips that utter them daily? Do our intentions and actions bespeak the sincerity of our prayer?

CHAPTER VI.

THAT THE SECOND OBJECT OF MAN'S DEVOTION SHOULD BE HIS OWN SANCTIFICATION. THE REASONS WHY HE SHOULD SEEK IT.

THE second object of the truly devoted man is his own sanctification. He wishes it effectually, not as an embellishment and as a perfection of his soul, but as something which God has commanded, which is pleasing to him, and which contributes to his glory. It is not to please himself in his virtues that he endeavors to acquire them, but to please God. Indeed, he is not anxious to know even if he is pleasing God; but acting with uprightness and simplicity, he looks not for any testimony to be given him of the worth of his actions.

In like manner, if he carefully shuns every sin and every imperfection, it is not merely because it is a stain and a deformity of the soul, but because it is an offence against God; a disorder that displeases the infinite holiness and purity of his looks; an object that is odious to him, and which provokes his indignation. Thus, while he is sorry with respect to God for a fault committed, he is well pleased with the feeling of shame and humiliation which this fault occasions in him.

He aims at holiness, not to appropriate it to himself nor to possess it as his own property, but to offer it in homage to God, to give to him all the glory of it as to the only source of holiness.

He wishes to become a saint, not in his own way and according to his own ideas, but according to the views and the ideas of God. He is not ignorant that his sanctification is much more the work of God than his own; that far from being able of himself to do anything towards it, he would only spoil the work were he to attempt to begin it. He knows that God must begin, continue, and finish the work; that his part is only to leave the whole to the great Artificer, to put no obstacle in the way, and to second the design of the First Mover by his consent and co-operation.

Finally, he is not led to aspire to a sublime holiness by a false elevation of sentiment, or by a jealous emulation of certain privileged souls; but he only wishes to fill up the measure of holiness to which God calls him; to correspond with the graces which he has received, and to be faithful according to the extent of the degree he is in: as well pleased at having received but one talent, provided he makes good use of it, as if he had received two or even five.

CHAPTER VII.

THE THIRD OBJECT OF DEVOTION: OUR HAPPINESS.

THE third object of devotion, that which interests us the most, is our own happiness. It is inseparably annexed to our being devoted to God. To be happy is to be united to the Sovereign Good; and devotion commences this union here below, in order to consummate it in eternity. Our happiness is also a necessary consequence of our sanctification; for it is a fixed principle, that what tends to render the soul better tends on that very account to render it happier. Perfection and happiness are linked together as cause and effect. This is true even with regard to God, in whom happiness is not so much a perfection as it is the result of his infinite perfections. It is, therefore, incontestable that devotion, rightly understood and rightly practised, is the source, and the only source, of the solid happiness that man can enjoy on earth.

But this transient happiness is but a mere shadow when compared to the eternal beatitude promised by God to those who have been devoted to him. In providing for his own glory he has not neglected our welfare; on the contrary, he will have our interest to depend on his glory, and that, in our submission to his will, we should find all the advantages of both this and the life to come. If devotion does not always produce such an effect here below, the fault is not to be attributed to it, but to those who misconceive its nature and err in its practice.

In the all-just and the infinitely simple ideas of the divine mind, our sanctification and happiness are reduced to God's glory, and are blended with it. Where

God sees the glory which he expects from us, there he sees our holiness, there our happiness. For this reason the truly devoted man considers his sanctification as only a means of glorifying God, and his own happiness as included in that glory of God of which it is the consequence. Thus he makes this glory his principal object and the chief end of his actions from this conviction that, even without thinking of it especially, he will become holy and happy in proportion as he promotes God's glory. He does not exclude the other two objects—God forbid! He even thinks of them often; but the first prevails and overshadows, as it were, the other two.

It is not so with the ordinary devout man. The object to which he gives the preference and his greatest attention is his salvation. He has only this view in mind; he does what he thinks proper to assure it; he shuns what he judges may expose it to danger. This is the measure of his holiness, and beyond it he hardly proceeds. As to the glory of God, he seldom acts directly for that end, though he will admit of nothing that may be opposed to it. Thus does the love of his own interest, which he considers above everything else, induce him to invert the order in which God wishes him to put these three objects. From thence arise all the defects of his devotion.

CHAPTER VIII.

QUALITIES OF TRUE DEVOTION TO GOD. OF THE SPIRIT OF PRAYER.

LET us come to the detail of the qualities which characterize devotedness to God. No one is ignorant that devotion is supernatural, in what light soever we may view it: supernatural in its object, which is God, known, not merely by reason, but by faith; supernatural in its motives, in its means, and in its end; supernatural inasmuch as it is impossible for man to conceive the idea of it by the mere light of his reason, or to embrace it by the power of his will alone, or to put it in practice by his own strength only; supernatural because far from being favorable in any thing to corrupt nature, it combats it, and aims at reforming it.

We can only, therefore, be drawn to devotion by the action of grace, which enlightens the mind, solicits the will, and strengthens the free-will. We can only maintain ourselves in it, advance in it, or attain to the perfection of it, by the help of grace.

And as, exclusive of certain graces which entirely precede the action of the soul, God grants others only by means of prayer; it follows, that the first thing that devotion inspires is an attraction for prayer; or, rather, it is itself that "spirit of grace and of prayer" which God promises by his prophet * "to pour out upon" his people. It is a "spirit of prayer," that is to say, a disposition, an habitual tendency of the soul, to rise up towards God and to unite itself to him,

* Zach. xii. 10.

by adoring his supreme majesty, by giving thanks for his blessings, by asking pardon for past offences, by soliciting the helps which are needful to our weakness. It is a "spirit of grace," because this disposition and this tendency are the effect of grace.

I say an habitual disposition which always subsists in the depth of the will, which constantly keeps it bent towards God, and which, as occasion or need requires, forms positive and formal acts, that are expressed by word of mouth or by the heart. These positive acts cannot be continual; but the interior affection, which produces and animates them, may and ought to be so. And it is this habitual elevation of the soul to God which is meant by the precept of Jesus Christ, "that we ought always to pray, and not to faint."*

* Luke xviii. 1.

If you have this spirit of prayer, Christian reader, you have true devotion. But you have it not yet if you are led to pray only by duty or necessity, and not by relish and desire. You do not possess it if the exercise of it be painful and repugnant to you; if it cost you a great effort; if you find it irksome, and are listless, tepid, and wilfully distracted in it; if you count the moments; if you curtail it as much as you can; in short, if you pay God as a bad debtor pays his debts. We may in this manner say many prayers, through habit, human respect, and by rote—because the rule or our state of life demands it—without having the spirit of prayer; nothing is more common.

CHAPTER IX.

THAT DEVOTION TO BE TRUE MUST BE INTERIOR.

THE spirit of prayer is evidently an interior spirit, because it is a spirit of grace; the "Spirit which asketh for us with unspeakable groanings; the Spirit of the Son, which God has sent into our hearts, crying Abba, Father;"* that is to say, implanting in us a filial affection, which is like a continual cry of the heart towards God our Father. This divine Spirit dwells in the inmost recesses of the soul, deeper than all else; and it is upon the noblest faculties of the soul—on our understanding, our will, and our liberty—that it exercises its power. True devotion, therefore, is essentially interior: it

* Rom. viii. 26 ; Gal. iv. 6.

resides in the very depths of the heart, whence it inspires good thoughts and sentiments. From within it diffuses itself without, and gives life to all the exterior works of piety.

What, indeed, would be a devotion merely exterior which consisted only in words and vain protestations or, at most, in actions that did not proceed from the heart? It would be but a phantom of devotion, which might deceive men who judge only from appearances, but which could not deceive God, whose eye penetrates the heart. Provided one renders useful services, men pay little attention to the good-will of him who serves them. But what need has God of our homage? It is only pleasing to him inasmuch as it tends to his glory, and it alone conduces to his glory when it is sincere and springs from the heart.

Devotion is also interior because it withdraws the soul from the exterior objects that cause distraction, bringing it back to itself and concentrating it in God, who causes his presence to be felt within. Hence, devotion teaches the soul to restrain the senses, to regulate the imagination, to suppress vain thoughts, to quiet emotions, to restrict its desires and to collect all its strength, in order to keep itself united to the object to which it is devoted. By this interior union with God, the soul sanctifies not only its vocal and mental prayers, not only the practice of its duties and good works, but also all animal actions, such as eating, drinking, sleeping, and such as seem to be the most indifferent, as conversations and proper recreation, all of which it refers to the glory of God, according to the advice of the Apostle.*

Devotion gives an experimental knowledge of that saying of Christ, "The kingdom of God is within you,"† words of

---

* 1 Cor. x. 31. † Luke xvii. 21.

which no one can comprehend the meaning but he who is truly devout. God, by the operation of his grace, exercises this dominion over the soul which is devoted to him, and renders it attentive to his voice, by which, at every instant, he makes known to it his will. And as this voice is infinitely delicate, and as it cannot be heard in the distraction, the tumult, and the excitement of the passions, the soul that has once felt its charms, and knows how beneficial it is to be docile to it, studies to keep itself in recollection, in calmness, in certain interior solitude, and in the greatest attention, that it may lose none of the instructions and admonitions which God may give. Thus a servant devoted to his master, and who is always ready to do his will, never permits himself to be distracted by other matters; he is attentive to the master's words, tries to understand them, observes his looks, his gestures, and the smallest sign of his wishes.

This attention should be continual, since the action of grace on the soul is continual. It is a thread that directs the soul and which it must constantly keep in hand, and which it cannot let go for a moment without going astray. Thus whosoever has seriously given himself to God experiences that his interior admonitions are continual and are very sensibly felt until he has acquired a habit of acting in all by the spirit of grace. Then this spirit having become familiar, and as it were natural, he follows it almost without being conscious of it, but its influence on all his actions is only greater.

Should it be objected, that so close and continued an attention must be very painful, I answer, in the first place, that a truly devout man will never make such an objection,—it would never even occur to him. This is clear to every one who understands the meaning of being devoted to God. I answer, in the second place, that if it be painful, it is sweetened by love, and that habit makes easy that which cost much in the beginning.

CHAPTER X.

THAT DEVOTION SHOULD APPEAR IN EXTERNAL ACTIONS.—REASONS WHICH PROVE THIS.

IT would, however, be a gross illusion to imagine that devotion should be wholly interior, and, under pretence that God looks within, to suppress vocal prayer and other external marks of piety. We are men, not pure spirits. It is proper that the body should share in the homage of the soul, and that our chief organs should be employed in the praises of God. We have received them for this purpose, and it is the noblest use we can make of them. The whole man should adore and pray.

Besides, the soul itself stands in need of being roused and supported in its piety by what affects the senses. Hence the external accessories of worship, the order and the majesty of the ceremonies, the variations and harmony of music, the sight of pictures and of other pious objects, are necessary means to entertain devotion. The respectful and humble posture of the body, the bended knee, the folded hands, the eyes modestly cast down or raised up towards Heaven, are so many expressions of reverence and attention of the soul in prayer, which naturally and imperceptibly lead it to accompany its feelings with these external signs.

Add to this the edification which we owe to our neighbor, who can only judge of our piety from what appears externally. Again, as religion is the first bond of society, it exacts a common, public, and consequently an external worship, in which men address the same supplications and offer the same prayers to God, and animate one another to sing his praises. The ecclesiastical ministry, which is of divine institution, is also an evident proof of the necessity of an external worship.

There was never one truly devout, even in the greatest solitude, who had not stated times in the day for vocal prayer. The interior spirit itself inspires even those who are the most contemplative to make use of such prayers.

Whether, therefore, we pray to God in public or in private, we should so attend to mental prayer as not to omit that which is vocal. The former could not long be kept up without the latter, and would infallibly degenerate into a proud and dangerous idleness. It is as difficult to discharge properly the duty of vocal prayer, unless it be joined to the practice of mental prayer,—which is the source from whence the interior spirit flows,—as it is difficult for the soul to support itself in pure contemplation without the occasional aid of vocal prayer. Even in contemplation, the soul frequently expresses its affections and transports by words, looks, sighs, tears, and other motions which are almost forced from it; and this proceeds from the union of soul and body and from their mutual correspondence.

CHAPTER XI.

THE ERROR OF THOSE WHO EXCLUDE MENTAL PRAYER FROM DEVOTION.

IF it be an abuse to exclude vocal prayer from devotion, it is a much more common fault to banish from it mental prayer. This may be excusable in coarse and ignorant people, who hardly make use of their reason, as also in the first heat of youth, in whom the extreme levity of the imagination needs to be fixed by some sensible object. But is it pardonable in persons of riper years, and who are better informed, not to know how to pray but with a book in hand? to imagine that they are idle unless they move their lips, and that God does not hear them unless they articulate their petitions, often loud enough, too, to disturb those who are praying by them? How many pious women go to church, loaded with books, in which all their devotion is contained! You see them take up one after the other to seek a method of hearing mass, or for confession and communion. The acts and the formulas are ready drawn up, they have only to pronounce them; and provided they have omitted none, they think they have properly discharged their duty, and that God demands no more. Nevertheless, the least act formed by the heart, the slightest feeling of their own, would be more pleasing to God, and more beneficial to themselves. But their heart is cold, dry, and empty; it says nothing amidst this rapid flow of words.

In vain do they allege that prayers ready made move them and nourish their devotion. I can hardly believe it of those methodical acts, in which are expressed in fine language sentiments that are foreign to those who recite them, and perhaps to him who composed them. I admit that they move at first on account of their novelty, and that the imagination is affected by them much more than the heart. People tire after a time of forms that recur daily; they cease to make an impression, and they are repeated mechanically and by rote; then others are sought for which have no better effect. Soon all methods are exhausted and the poor soul knows not where to turn.

Why not begin early the habit of recollection—of seeking in the heart, as David did, the prayer which we wish to make to God,* of complaining to him of our coldness and insensibility, and of conjuring him to supply our spiritual poverty? Would it be praying wrongly humbly to acknowledge in God's presence our misery, to implore the assistance of his

* Ps. xviii. 15.

grace? and if, at intervals, we feel some good sentiments, to ascribe them with gratitude to the Author of all good?

When the source of devotion is in the heart, it is inexhaustible; the affections which flow from it continually vary, and produce each time a fresh delight. In order to express them there is no need of studied speeches; the simplest, the most natural, and the most lively expressions immediately present themselves. Even the silence of a heart touched and softened is more eloquent than words; and frequently it has no other resource than silence to show God all it feels.

Is it not clear that these methodical formulas of prayer encourage idleness and dispense with the preparation for prayer which the wise man enjoins?* The opening and reading of the book is all the preparation.

You must not speak to such people of

* Ecclus. xviii. 23.

meditation. They cannot meditate, they say; their head will not bear it. I own that meditation is painful to those who are not used to reflect; that lively imaginations are little suited for it, and that few are capable of continuing it for a great length of time. Should they be advised to drop all reflections once they are in the presence of God, and to pass quickly to the affections, they will answer that their will is not easily moved; that if they have a good thought it soon vanishes, and on this account they make use of books.

If you tell them to keep themselves at rest, and gently to draw down the dew from heaven by fervid and short acts, repeated from time to time, they condemn this rest as a state of idleness, and express their aversion to this manner of prayer; yet this is the prayer of interior souls. Hence, they are not interior, and they dread to be so. Still, they flatter themselves that they are devout, because they speak much and for a long time with God; but this only serves to fatigue their lungs without inflaming the heart.

Let them say what they will, self-love guides their prayers; they pray more to please themselves than to please God. Their object is to bear witness to themselves that they have prayed; and they think they have a palpable proof of it when they have recited so many forms of prayer that they lose their breath. For the same reason many speak aloud, that the ear may be an additional witness. St. Anthony, who doubtless was truly devout, was not of this way of thinking; for being asked which was the best manner of praying, he answered, "It is when we pray without being aware of it."

CHAPTER XII.

THAT IT IS AN ABUSE TO MULTIPLY TOO MUCH THE PRACTICES OF DEVOTION.

ANOTHER abuse of external devotion is that of multiplying its practices so much that the day is hardly long enough to finish them. The old methods are kept and new ones daily assumed. This constrains the mind and encroaches on its liberty; it often trenches on the duties of one's state of life, as action is left for prayer; or if both are tried at once, the attention is so divided that neither is done as it should be. It is certainly good to intermix some ejaculatory prayers with our occupations, and now and then to suspend our work, in order to recollect one's self in God. But such prayers should be short, and come rather from the heart than the lips.

Some persons whom I have seen here* place all their devotion in remaining a long time in church, in running to hear sermons, in being present at every Benediction, and in not missing any indulgence. They have a calendar where all the feasts celebrated in different Communities are marked, and they consider it a sacrifice when they are not present at each and every one. They join every possible sodality and all the different associations, and hence they are burdened with so many practices and prayers, that they need a confessor to relieve them, if they are not so much attached to them that they will not consent to give up a single one.

Their intention is good. Each of these practices of itself is good, but there is

*[The author speaks of Paris, where he was living when he wrote this book.—THE EDITOR.]

need of moderation in everything, and in pious exercises and practices more than in anything else. Neither the mind nor the heart is kept busy by such an accumulation of practices. The imagination alone is exercised, and how lively, ardent, and unstable it is, especially among devout persons, is well known. If the interior spirit did nothing else but regulate this excess, and give rise to a devotion which is orderly, moderate, and reasonable, it would be a sufficient reason to engage pious souls to embrace it.

CHAPTER XIII.

THAT WE MUST GIVE OURSELVES UP TO GOD WITHOUT RESTRICTION AND WITHOUT RESERVE.

TRUE devotion admits of no reserve. It consists in surrendering ourselves wholly to grace, and in being resolved to go as far as it will lead us. This absolute surrender to grace consists in removing all the obstacles which are a hindrance to its action as soon as we know them; in following it step by step with an exact fidelity, and never anticipating it, nor rushing into any of the excesses of an indiscreet fervor. People are liable to this fault in the first transports of their ardor. Several saints have blamed themselves for it, and in particular St. Bernard, who ruined his stomach at an early period by excessive abstinence. There is also often in this temptation of the devil, who, on our entering the spiritual career, endeavors to exhaust our strength, that he may prevent us from finishing it, and even make us turn back. We shall, however, be in no danger of falling if, in regard to fasting, vigils, and especially corporal penance, we consult a wise director and follow his advice.

But in every other respect, it is clear that to make terms with God, to be unwilling to use violence with ourselves only up to a certain point, to set bounds to our spiritual course, and to resolve not to exceed them, is not to devote ourselves to God, but to give ourselves to him with measure and restriction. In our devotedness to man, it is necessary that there should always be reserve; for at least the rights of God must always be excepted. But as God is infinitely superior to all that exists, and as nothing can limit the exercise of his dominion over his creatures, his service is not, of itself, susceptible of any reserve; and whosoever embraces it should embrace it without exception or condition. For to devote ourselves to him is to engage ourselves to acknowledge no other law than his supreme will, and to conform ourselves to it, how painful soever it may be to nature.

Neither must we allege our weakness, and say, I never could do this or that, even though grace should demand it of me. The will of God renders possible whatever it commands, because it always joins to the command the means of accomplishing it. God would be unjust if, when wishing us to do something, he did not give us sufficient assistance to do it, since of ourselves we can do nothing. You read of certain heroic deeds in the lives of the saints; and whilst you admire them, you despair of imitating them. But how do you know that God will demand such things of you? and if he should, why could you not do with his grace what this one and that one did? Be not, therefore, dismayed; what appears to you to-day absolutely impracticable will seem to you, if not easy, at least very possible, when the time for action comes.

It is not always a bad will that prompts us to make these secret reserves when we engage in the path of devotion. If it were, I would not hesitate to say that such a devotion would be false and illusive; that we should evidently expose ourselves to fail in our engagements, as God owes us no graces for serving him in our own way; and that we should hazard even our salvation, howsoever desirous we might be of securing it. The usual cause of these reserves is, that, seeing before us the vast career of sanctity, and consulting only our present strength, we judge ourselves incapable of continuing to the end. We, therefore, enter upon it because we are of good will; but we form a plan to ourselves, conformable to our actual weakness, to which we mean to confine ourselves without going farther.

This is a gross error which proceeds partly from ignorance, partly from self-love desirous to spare itself, and partly also from the devil, who is jealous of our progress. We ought to bear in mind that grace is the only source of our strength; that it will increase in proportion as we are faithful; that God always measures the greatness of his helps by the greatness of the difficulties: so that, the more we advance, the greater is our ardor to run, and the more easily we surmount obstacles. What should we say of a child who, not reflecting that his strength will insensibly increase with age, should measure, according to his present weakness, the burden which he is to carry when he becomes a man, and would not believe that he then could carry twenty times more?

Whosoever you may be, then, who mean to give yourself to God, give yourself to him wholly and entirely. Do not make terms with him. Fear but one thing,—that of not being generous enough. Be persuaded that the least reserve will weaken you, even in those things which you freely consent to do; and, on the contrary, your burden will be the lighter the less you seek to diminish it. This will seem a paradox only to him who does not consider that God displays all the power of his grace in favor of a noble and generous soul, who spares no pains to please him; and that a narrow and contracted heart constrains him, in spite of himself, to use reserve on his part.

It is not my purpose to explain, in detail, what it is to have no reserve with God, nor what kinds of reserve are openly or secretly blended with most devotions: this would exceed the narrow limits of this work. Practice will teach souls of good will more than it would be possible for me to say.

CHAPTER XIV.

THAT TRUE DEVOTION ADMITS OF NO DIVISION.

TRUE devotion admits of no division—"The Lord thy God shalt thou adore, and him only shalt thou serve."* Such is the law of devotedness. Adoration, which comprises the homage of the mind and of the heart, excludes all reserve; and the service which belongs to God alone excludes all division. Every other service besides his is only lawful inasmuch as it flows from and depends upon his service. Christ has declared that no one can serve two masters,† such as God and the world, whose wills are contrary, whose laws are opposed to one another, and consequently whose service is incompatible. God wants

---

* Matt. iv. 10. † Matt. vi. 24.

all for himself; the world also wants all for itself. There is no possibility of reconciling their pretensions, which are mutually destructive of each other. I, therefore, must make a choice, and if I love the one, I must hate the other; if I obey one, I must despise the orders of the other.

How is it possible to misapprehend so obvious a truth? And yet almost all who aim at devotion undertake to reconcile the interests of God with those of the world; they pretend to unite in the same heart the love of God and the love of the world, and by wishing to belong to both they belong to neither. We might say of all such what the prophet Elias said to the Israelites: "How long do you halt between two sides? If the Lord be God, follow him; but if Baal, then follow him."*

People think that they no longer side with the world because they have re-

* 3 Kings xviii. 21.

nounced what is criminal and evidently dangerous in it. They are no longer slaves to voluptuousness, which is the chief divinity of the world; but they are still slaves to interest and false honor. They follow in regard to these two objects the maxims which are reproved by the Gospel, making a great account of riches, of nobility, of dignities, of whatever elevates and distinguishes them; loving or desiring these things, either for themselves or for those dear to them; envying them in others and using every endeavor to preserve them or to acquire them. On a thousand occasions they adopt the judgment of the world and conform their conduct to it. They are jealous of its esteem and are afraid of losing it by declaring themselves too openly in favor of piety, and they retain it at the expense of virtue in spite of the reproaches of their conscience. They dread its censure and ridicule, and they manage to shield themselves from it; thereby the service of God suffers. They are tormented and violently drawn on both sides; human respect enslaves them and keeps them continually in mortal agonies. They wish to belong to God, and blush at being thought to belong to him; they pray to him by stealth, and as carefully conceal themselves in the discharge of their duties of piety as if they were doing some bad action. What slavery! What torment! But, at the same time, what infidelity, what cowardice, what perfidy!

Is this being devoted to God? Does he then deserve to be served only in secret? Is it a shame to acknowledge him for our Master? They do not wish to attract notice, they say. If by this they mean making parade of their devotion, displaying it with pomp and ostentation, seeking to be seen and applauded in the good works they do, they are right, and

they observe the precept of the Gospel.*
But between such display and trembling through fear of being looked upon as a servant of God—as one devoted to the glory and the interests of so great and so good a Master—there is a middle way. This consists in going on freely and frankly in our duties, without taking heed whether we be noticed or not; in following the dictates of our conscience uprightly; in paying to God, without affectation, but always openly, the homage which he expects from us for his own glory and for the edification of our neighbor, and in doing in secret only that which he himself wishes that we should conceal from others.†

The truly devout man well knows how to keep this middle path. He is not afraid to have it known that he serves God with all his heart, and that he holds

---

* Matt. vi. 18. † Ibid.

the world in contempt and abhorrence. He plainly expresses this when and where it is necessary, and when he ought to trample under foot all human respect. But he is not less careful to conceal certain practices of piety, certain good works, of which he wishes that God alone should be witness. Thus does he reconcile what Jesus Christ says: "So let your light shine before men, that they may see your good works, and glorify your Father who is in heaven," * and what he says in another place: "When you pray you shall not be as the hypocrites, that love to stand and pray in the synagogues and corners of the streets, that they may be seen by men. But enter into thy chamber, and, having shut the door, pray to thy Father in secret." † He has always in his mind the sentence pronounced by our Saviour: "Every one

---

*Matt. v. 16.   † Matt. vi. 5,

that shall confess me before men, I will also confess him before my Father; but he that shall deny me before men, I will also deny him before my Father."*

I know that there are cases in which prudence authorizes caution. A feeble virtue should not be exposed too openly, or brave human respect too boldly, at the hazard of yielding to the assaults that may be made upon it. There are cases where the deference which is due to a father, to a husband, to a master, who may be unfavorable to piety, requires that we should carefully hide from them what might offend or irritate them. This was the practice among the early Christians in their domestic persecutions. For the sake of peace they did not declare themselves to their parents, their masters, or their pagan friends; the brother shunned the look of his brother who was

* Matt. x. 32.

watching him, the wife that of her husband, and, in general, the faithful that of the unbeliever. To-day, more than ever, there are occasions in which we ought to observe the same line of conduct. About this we should consult a prudent confessor and follow his advice.

But when we are not responsible to any one for our actions, and the most we have to fear is the powerless censure of the worldly, we should not hesitate to bid it defiance, boldly to stand up, and openly to declare what we are, and what we mean to be. Are the partisans of the world afraid to show themselves? Were we ourselves afraid when we were of that number? The shortest way is to break with the world absolutely, heart and will; to assume a manner of seeing, judging, speaking, and of acting entirely opposed to it; to have no other relations with it than those which are indispensable and compatible with the most delicate piety, and in other respects to renounce its commerce, its pleasures, its esteem; to be above its censures, and to rejoice like the Apostles* and all the true disciples of Jesus Christ, that it should criticise, blame, despise, calumniate, and persecute us.

Our devotedness to God demands these dispositions of us, and it will produce them in us if it be sincere. When one has taken this part with resolution, he is soon rewarded, even in this life. He is loosed from many chains, outwardly free and inwardly at peace. God is satisfied, conscience makes no reproaches, and the world itself admires and approves the contempt he has for it.

* Acts v. 41.

CHAPTER XV.

THAT DEVOTION IS FOR PERSONS OF EVERY AGE.

TRUE devotion belongs to every age and to every condition; it extends to every situation and to every action in life.

As soon as the Christian comes to the first use of reason, he is bound to consecrate to God his earliest thoughts and his budding affections. It is of these first-fruits God is the most jealous, as right order demands that the devotedness of our childhood to God should be the first-fruit of the development of the soul. In that happy age when all is candor and innocence, the more the mind is disengaged from prejudices, the more the heart is free from passion, the purer is the conscience, the more also is the child susceptible of a sincere, tender, simple, and ingenuous piety. "Suffer the little children to come unto me,"* said Christ. They are unconscious of malice; the world has not seduced nor perverted them; they are free from all stain; their newly-created soul is flexible to all the movements of grace. The kingdom of heaven is so adapted to them that, in a more advanced age, in order to enter into it, we must become as much as possible little children.

Ye young hearts, give yourselves, therefore, to God, and respond to his sweet invitations. You are affected by the caresses of a father and of a mother; make trial of the caresses of your heavenly Father. It is to you particularly that it is said: "Taste and see how sweet the Lord is."† Let yourselves be early in-

---

* Mark x. 14. † Ps. xxxiii. 9.

ebriated with his divine love. This will preserve you from the flattering but poisoned liquor which the world will one day put before you.

And you parents, and you who have the charge of children or direct their consciences, hasten to bend them under the yoke of the Lord. It is good to have carried it from the earliest years; the soul then is easily fashioned to it, and should it in future unfortunately shake it off, it will more readily take it upon itself again.

The more we advance in the light of reason, the less excusable we are in refusing to devote ourselves to God. The passions, it is true, begin to solicit indulgence, and their tumultuous clamors tend to drown the voice of grace; but in their first uprisings they are easily silenced, or, at least, it is easy to preserve the heart from their seduction: pious practices, good books, good instructions and examples, and a frequent use of the sacraments, will baffle all their attempts.

The age of manhood, when reason is in its vigor, the heart more consistent and the character more settled, would be the fittest time for grace to act upon the soul and incline it to devotion, if the cares of life, the thorns of ambition, and bad habits formerly contracted, were not obstacles. But there is no obstacle which an upright mind and a resolute will may not overcome. Upon what plausible pretext can a Christian dispense with devoting himself to God, in that period of life in which he sees more clearly than ever the necessity and the advantages of so doing? If he be then more seriously taken up with his temporal concerns, is it not just that he should think of that permanent settlement which his labor ought to procure for him in heaven? that he should direct to that object, which is the only one of real importance, all his projects and all his designs?

In old age, when the passions, having become extinct, leave the mind in possession of its lights, and no longer thwart the determinations of the will; when experience has dispelled the charms and illusions of the world; when objects make but a faint impression on the enfeebled senses; when infirmities and decay warn us of an approaching dissolution, and that we are on the brink of eternity,— everything invites, everything urges us to give to God the last moments at least of life, and repair, as far as can be, by a fervent and solid piety, the loss of so many years of which we have robbed him by a shameful and perhaps criminal course. There is no more time for delay, death is rapidly approaching; it will be too late when the last sickness surprises us.

The levity of childhood, the impetuosity of youth, the private and public occupations of riper years, the debility of old age cannot, then, be considered as reasons for dispensation, or any excuse. Hence we cannot but conclude that every age has its own difficulties, and that, in every stage of life, if we mean to belong to God, we must do violence to ourselves.

CHAPTER XVI.

THAT DEVOTION EXTENDS TO ALL CONDITIONS OF LIFE.

THE same judgment must be formed of the various states in society. Each one offers a favorable and unfavorable side to devotion, and none has any just cause for exemption. Greatness has its dangers for salvation, from which no one can be preserved without God's special protection,—a protection we have no right to expect but in proportion to our devotedness to his service. Offices of public trust bring great obligations, and expose us to great temptations. How can we expect to discharge these duties and overcome these temptations without solid devotion? Cares and occupations multiply and hardly leave us time to breathe; but, if the heart be with God, we shall find ourselves free in the midst of all these troubles, they will even become so many occasions of testifying our obedience and our love.

How many have sanctified themselves in military life, where the obstacles seem insurmountable! How many in the magistracy! How many even whilst intrusted with the public funds! I except, indeed, some states in themselves opposed to salvation and proscribed by the Gospel, in which no one is obliged to engage, and which are only tolerated in well-regulated governments. But, such excepted, I boldly advance that there is no state of life in which saints have not been formed, and actually are formed to-day. Would God, the Author of the different states of society, have established one in which it were morally impossible to be saved? If in some there are greater difficulties, there he has given greater help, as all those who have abandoned themselves to his guidance have happily experienced.

Devotion is also suited to every situation. It is equally beneficial and equally necessary in health and in sickness, in prosperity and in adversity, in wealth and inp overty, in joy and in sadness, amid the good things of this life and when overwhelmed with its evils;—amid the good things that we may guard against their abuse, amid evils that we may be enabled to support them. As these evils are incomparably more common here below than the good things, and as all human resources are ofttimes insufficient, it follows that devotedness and submission to the holy will of God are the only solid comfort which remain to a Christian amidst afflictions and crosses, whatsoever may be their nature.

Finally, devotion, by its very nature, extends to every action; and there is not one which it is not calculated to sanctify. It would not be a perfect devotedness, did it not subject to God's dominion whatever can be subjected to it. Now, such are all our free actions called by moralists "human actions." It is God's intention that they all be referred to him, and that they be done for his glory. Therefore, the truly devoted man consecrates them all to him without exception, and by this consecration sanctifies them. He knows that where a rational being should act according to reason, a Christian should act according to religion; that it is not sufficient to act in the state of grace, but that he moreover ought to act in addition through a principle of grace; just as, in order to act reasonably, it is not enough for a man to have the use of reason, but he must apply it to what he actually does. This principle, which is unquestionably true, will lead us a great way, if we take pains to examine it.

It therefore is a mistake to fancy ourselves devoted because we daily acquit ourselves, almost by routine, of a certain number of pious exercises, whilst in other respects we live at our ease, indulging without restraint all kinds of thoughts, actions, and desires, provided they have nothing criminal in them. God, in this way, would only be attended to at certain times in the day, and the rest would be at our own disposal. But this is not as it should be. Every moment belongs to him; and he will have us employ all our time in a manner worthy of him and of our Christian profession. We are not at liberty to dispose of time at our own pleasure; to waste it, for instance, in visits, in frivolous conversations, in books of mere amusement, or in a slothful indolence. The duties of our state in life, our work, and some short relaxation that may be allowed to nature, ought to fill up the vacant hours of the day; but nothing ought to interrupt that incessant prayer of the heart, which Jesus Christ and the Apostle have recommended to us. The object of prescribed prayers is to draw down the blessing of God upon our actions, in which his grace is the more necessary the more we are exposed to dissipation, to act from merely human impulse, and to commit many faults which often escape our notice.

CHAPTER XVII.

THAT LOVE IS THE ONLY FOUNDATION OF DEVOTION.

LOVE alone can produce devotedness. It is love that gives it birth, growth, and perfection; and the practice of devotedness in turn nourishes and strengthens love. We may define devotion, "the love of God reduced to practice." What would that devotedness be that did not have as its principal cause the love of the object to which we devote ourselves? And if a man can only be devoted to his fellow-man inasmuch as he gives him his affection, warmly espouses his interest, eagerly seeks every occasion of obliging and pleasing him, not sparing for his sake rest, health, property, nor even life; how much more affectionate, more eager, more ardent and generous ought the sentiments of a soul be that is devoted to God!

When He commands us to love him with all our heart, with all our soul, with all our strength, does he not equivalently command us to be entirely devoted to him? Devotion is literally the practice of the great precept of the love of God; a failure in devotion is a failure in the observance of this precept; and we may apply to devotion what is said of love of God, that it is "the fulfilling of the law."*

Hence perfect devotion, like "perfect charity, casteth out fear." † Devotion is characteristic of children, as fear is of slaves. Fear sees in God a Master, a Judge, an Avenger, and serves him in this character; devotion sees in him a Father whom it fears, respects, and obeys, because it loves him. Fear may dispose a

---

* Rom. xiii. 10. † 1 John iv. 18.

soul to become devoted, but it does not make it such; and as soon as it is devoted, love, not fear, prevails. Now love, wherever it prevails, aims at absolute empire, and banishes fear, which is totally opposed to it. For fear springs from self-love, which is the enemy of the love of God and the bane of devotion.

What, then, is to be thought of those who serve God through the fear of being lost, who are only struck with the terrible truths of religion, and who are continually chilled with gloomy apprehensions? To whom are they devoted? to God? No; to themselves and to their own interest. Why do they dread sin? because it offends God? By no means; it is because God punishes it. Why do they fear hell? on account of the pain of loss or the eternal privation of God? Not at all; the pain of sense, the eternal flames, is that alone which terrifies them.

Let us not, however, confound the

terror which springs from a lively and weak imagination, and which the heart disowns, with the fear which proceeds from mean and servile sentiments. Many truly devoted souls are subject to this terror, which is their torment, and which they find great difficulty in overcoming; but it lessens as they advance in devotion, and at last it wholly disappears. It is not uncommon that, after having been terrified all their lifetime at the judgments of God, they die in peace, confidence, and security.

CHAPTER XVIII.

THAT TO BE TRULY DEVOTED WE MUST FORGET OUR OWN INTERESTS, AND SEEK GOD ALONE.

FOR the same reason, true devotion is not mercenary nor interested. At first, indeed, when God lavishes upon the soul his consolations, it becomes too much attached to them; it seeks them, and this is one of the motives of its fidelity. But it soon lifts itself above these caresses; and when God has weaned it from them, it does not serve him with less zeal and exactness. The devoted Christian on entering this career becomes a little child; God treats him as such, it would not be fair to ascribe to him mercenary views, because in that state consolations are his attraction and delight.

With regard to salvation, whatever progress the soul may have made in devotion, it always desires it, and it rejects with horror any indifference to this essential end; but it desires it less on its own account than on account of God. It wishes its own happiness,—how could it not wish it? But it wishes still more the glory of God and the accomplishment of his holy will. It serves him, like David, "for the reward;"* but that is only a secondary motive; the first and the principal motive is love. He who loves purely views the object he loves with a direct regard which does not fall back upon its own interest. He does not exclude it, and he even cannot exclude it, because he places his happiness in the possession of what he loves. But he does not establish his end in this possession because it renders him happy; he estab-

---

*Ps. cxviii. 112.

lishes it in the glory which results from it to God, and in the fulfilling of his will.

I shall not enlarge further on the delicacy and the extreme purity of the divine love; but if we attentively reflect on the qualities of the devotedness which has God for its object, we shall understand how free it ought to be from every interested view. I know not to what heights it reaches upon earth in some privileged souls—they only can tell—but it is certain that no interested views nor self-satisfaction can dwell in the abode of the blessed; and it is this which completes their happiness. This is a truth incomprehensible to self-love,—a truth which throws it into desolation and despair, because it cannot form an idea of a happiness in which it has no share, and from which it is totally excluded.

All devotion, if it be solid, and if love be its principle, aims at this admirable purity which characterizes the citizens of heaven, and if it cannot attain to it, it strives at least to approach it. Let us examine if our devotion be such. Let us not be afraid of sounding its motives, and with the help of grace let us labor to purify them. For the fear of being lost, let us substitute the fear of losing God; for the interested desire of saving ourselves, let us substitute that of possessing God and of being eternally united to him. Substantially, it is the same thing. The object is not changed, but the manner of regarding it is very different; and it is this difference of view and of motive which gives to devotion various degrees of excellency and perfection.

CHAPTER XIX.

FATAL EFFECTS OF SELF-LOVE ON DEVOTION.

AFTER what has just been said, what becomes of all those devotions of which self-love is the basis? How false they are! How deceitful and yet how common! I do not speak of that gross self-love which is the parent of passions and vices. I speak of a spiritual self-love which glides artfully into pious practices, —of a self-love which has also its capital vices; which is proud, avaricious, envious, voluptuous, greedy, vindictive, and slothful; which is blind also, and the more dangerous as the objects to which it is attached are holy.

In fact, are those devoted people rare

who nourish a secret pride, and who, like the Pharisee in the Gospel, are full of self-esteem and contempt for their neighbor? who appropriate to themselves the graces and the gifts of God and dread nothing so much as to be stripped of them; who envy those whom they think to be more favored or more advanced; who relish with passion heavenly consolations; who are greedy of them and insatiable; who are passionate, full of hatred, gall, and malice, and all, as they imagine, through a zeal for God's cause; in short, who are given to remissness, effeminacy, idleness, and to all that is flattering to nature?

I own that in the beginning, and even in the progress of the spiritual life, we are more or less liable to these excesses on account of our natural imperfection. Self-love finding itself deprived of temporal comforts on entering into the path of piety, has recourse to those which are spiritual. It seizes them and desires to make them its prey, attaching itself to them all the more strongly as they are of a more excellent nature. But the man truly devoted constantly labors to oppose self-love, to pursue it from place to place and to dislodge it from every quarter where it may take refuge. This warfare is his main object, and he thinks that he fails if he relaxes ever so little or grows faint in his attacks. As the spirit of religion detaches a man from temporal things, the spirit of devotion detaches him from spiritual things, for it does not allow him to take complacency in them, nor to ascribe them to himself, nor to claim any right to them, but it leads him by degrees to renunciation—to divest himself of these objects and to be in perfect poverty with regard to them. He has everything and is attached to nothing. God gives and takes when and as he pleases; and he is neither afflicted nor elated.

The opposite vices do not show themselves at first on account of their subtlety; but in proportion as we advance, divine light teaches us to distinguish them, and all our fidelity consists in drawing down upon us this light, in receiving it with gratitude, and in using it for our amendment. Before we can entirely up root these delicate views, it will cost us long and painful efforts. We will stand in need of great courage; we must use extreme violence to ourselves,—it will be the work of our whole life. But at last, if we correspond with grace, we shall effect it, and we shall free ourselves as much as possible from the tyranny of self-love. God, who sees our good-will, by sending us merciful trials, will accomplish what of ourselves we could not do.

CHAPTER XX.

THAT DEVOTION GIVES BIRTH TO CONFIDENCE. THE GOOD EFFECTS AND NECESSITY OF THIS CONFIDENCE.

DEVOTION, being the daughter of love, is the mother of confidence; for the more we love God, the more we confide in him; the one is the rule and the measure of the other. The love of God is not a blind love, but a love founded on the knowledge of his infinite goodness towards his creatures. It is this knowledge which leads us to commit to him all our interests, never to mistrust him, to believe, in spite of his apparent rigor, that he means to save us, and that, in fact, he will save us if we preserve our confidence. "Throw yourself into his arms," says St. Augustin; "he will not withdraw and let you fall." I add to this thought of the holy Doctor, that, should he seem sometimes to withdraw himself from you, it is because he means to try you and to see how far your confidence will extend, in order to increase your reward. As this virtue is that which honors him the most, it is also that which he exercises the most, and in strong and generous souls he pushes the trial to the last extremity.

Confidence is a mean between two opposite vices—presumption and pusillanimity, both of which proceed from the same source—self-love. We are presumptuous when we rely too much on ourselves. We are pusillanimous when, relying only on ourselves, we realize how weak is our support. The presumptuous man says: "Nothing will ever shake me." The pusillanimous says, on the contrary: "The slightest breath will upset me." The man possessing confidence, considering himself, admits with the pusillanimous that a trifle can upset him; but, looking up to God, he adds that nothing is capable of shaking him. He thus unites both sentiments, which, being separately vicious, become a virtue when joined together.

Nothing is more necessary or more frequently in demand in the career of devotion than confidence. God delights in exercising our faith. He constrains us to shut our eyes and to walk in the dark. He apparently bewilders us, so that we no longer know where we are nor whither we are going. He makes us lose our foothold, takes from us all knowledge of our interior state, forbids us all reflection on ourselves; and, if we look out for any assurance, he leaves us a prey to the keenest anxiety. Why does he thus deal with us? To force us to renounce the conduct of ourselves and to abandon ourselves entirely to him.

What would become of faith, and of

what use would it be, were we always clearly to see the state of our soul; were we informed of the reasons for which God wills or permits the events which befall us from time to time, and were we able to trace step by step the way and the progress of his operations? The confidence of the blind man in his guide is grounded on the fact that he himself is not able to see. The more unknown to him the road through which he is led, and the more dangerous and surrounded with precipices, the greater is the confidence shown; and thus he shows no solicitude, he makes no inquiries, as he is confident of not being misled and of being safely conducted to his journey's end.

On our devoting ourselves to God, our confidence in him should be boundless. To withdraw it, under any pretence whatever, is to take ourselves back and to become our own leaders. To fix it within certain limits, which we are determined not to exceed, is to put a restriction to our devotedness. Now nothing is more injurious to God, or more prejudicial to our spiritual profit. Is it not to doubt the goodness of God or his infinite power to believe either that he will not or cannot rescue us from all the difficulties, and from the greatest dangers in which we engage ourselves upon his word and through a blind submission to his guidance? It is absolutely impossible that God should fail such a soul, and that he should not succor it opportunely; that would be to fail to himself. But it belongs to him alone to judge how far the trial is to go, and to mark the precise moment in which he will afford relief. Let us, therefore, abandon ourselves to him, and let us say with Job, "Although he should kill me, I will trust in him."*

* Job xiii. 51.

CHAPTER XXI.

THAT DEVOTION BEGETS SELF-KNOWLEDGE, AND CONSEQUENTLY HUMILITY.

DEVOTION does not lead less to self-knowledge than to the knowledge of God; and as confidence is the fruit of the knowledge of God, humility is likewise the fruit of the knowledge of one's self.

Man does not and cannot know himself well by the light of nature alone; and it is through the want of this knowledge that he is proud. But the moment he devotes himself to God a heavenly light shines upon him and opens his eyes; he begins to see himself such as he is,—full of miseries, weak, repugnant to all good, and prone to all evil. Recollection rendering him attentive to himself, he soon learns that he has two natures, one the enemy of the other, and that the spiritual life is but a series of combats in which he must engage and do violence to himself. Experience instructs him still better. On trial he finds how difficult it is to overcome himself and to struggle against his evil inclinations; how much time and labor it costs him to correct the smallest of the faults into which he frequently falls; how painful the practice of virtue is, however much be the love which he has conceived for it; what resistance he makes to grace; into what slothfulness, negligences, infidelities he falls daily; how frail his will is, how weak his resolutions, how fruitless his best desires; what power the world, the flesh, and the devil have over him; and how, without a special and continual assistance from God, he would fall at every instant.

This experimental knowledge of himself, joined to the lights he receives from above, inspires him with humility, which is nothing else but the consciousness and the intimate conviction of that unhappy fund of corruption which each one of us brings into the world, which age and occasions unfold, and which is the germ of our passions and vices. The more he advances the deeper becomes this conviction, and the more deeply is humility rooted in his heart.

Hence springs his contempt of himself, his salutary distrust of his own strength, the sincere preference which he gives to others over himself, believing them to be better than himself, or, at least, persuaded that if they had received the same graces they would have made a better use of them. Hence, also, arises that confusion which he feels at the sight of the favors God bestows on him, of the esteem and respect which are shown him, and of the praises which are given him. All this, instead of exalting him, abases and humbles him in his own eyes. If he reflects on himself, it is only to humble himself the more; he sees not his virtues, he is ignorant of his progress; to God alone he attributes his victories, and his failures to himself.

CHAPTER XXII.

SIMPLICITY AND THE FEAR OF BEING NOTICED ARE THE CHARACTERISTICS OF TRUE DEVOTION. HOW FEW POSSESS THEM.

TRUE devotion, when left to itself, walks in the simplest and most common path; it follows the beaten track, and shuns the by-ways. It abhors singularity, dreading to be observed and noticed; its disposition is to hide itself, and to be lost with the crowd. A friend to those virtues and practices which have the least show, and which upon that account are the more solid, it prefers them to all others. It is the lowly and timid violet, which dares not lift its head up to the light, but suffers itself to be trodden under foot in the grass that covers it. Except what is due to example and edification, it carefully conceals its conduct from the knowledge of others.

Devotion is perfectly natural; nothing indicates show nor affectation. Far from wishing for extraordinary gifts, it thinks itself unworthy of them, and constantly asks God to do nothing for it that may attract the attention of men, or give to it the slightest consideration. It is not envious of those saints who have signalized themselves by miracles, who have had visions, revelations, the gift of prophecy, and other singular graces, and who have been the wonder of their age. It admires and it reveres those in whom such gifts were conspicuous; but for its own part it chooses obscurity, contempt, ignominy, to be set at naught, to be known only from its failings, or to be altogether ignored and forgotten.

The good works which make a noise in

the world are not to its taste; it prefers those which have God alone for witness. It enjoins secrecy on those whom it befriends, and hides from them, as much as it can, the source of their benefits. It would hide it from itself, and not allow that its left hand knew what the right hand did; it loses the remembrance of its gifts, and would think it criminal to recall them or dwell on them with complacency.

Devoted people of this character are so rare, that one might think that I have been drawing a picture from fancy. Some, however, are to be found, and, because they have nothing to distinguish them, they are thought to be more rare than they really are. In many others you see only singularity, affectation, and ostentation. They have their own air, manner, and style of dressing, their language and conduct. Some of them aim at extraordinary kinds of prayer; they use vain efforts for that purpose; their imagination seduces them, the devil deceives them, and pride takes possession of them. They must have practices and prayers for themselves alone; they even disdain to unite their voices with those of the people to sing the praises of the Lord.

How many persons given to devotion there are who have fixed places at the church, as if in perspective, which favor their desire of distinction as well as of convenience! Observe how they pray, how much their exterior is studied, cramped, and forced. The solid and ordinary books of devotion are not those which they read; they seek mystical works which treat of the most elevated states; they satiate their curiosity with them, flattering themselves that they appreciate them, while in reality they do not understand them. All the profit they draw from such books is to retain certain singular phrases, which they glory in on certain occasions, giving themselves out as souls of the highest spirituality.

Who would imagine that so refined a pride could thus insinuate itself into piety? Who could imagine that people devoted themselves to God only to seek themselves; that they aimed at sanctity only to have the reputation of it; and that they placed all the fruit of virtue in approving themselves, and in winning the applause of others.

I do not say that all persons of this sort are hypocrites, or that these characteristics are applicable to each one of them in their full force. But I do say, with all truth, that very few ground their devotion on humility; that pride, the most subtle and most dangerous of all vices, is that against which we are the least on our guard; that it is incomparably the most dangerous; that no other vice is so apt to blind us; that it is the most deeply rooted in the heart of man, the most difficult to combat, and the last to be extirpated. I say that it is more to be apprehended by those who make profession of an exalted piety than by others, because it especially fastens on virtue. Indeed, it is the moth which corrodes and corrupts it, and we cannot guard too much against it. If we expel it from one place, it immediately enters into another.

Would you know what is the touchstone of true devotion? It is the love of humiliations. He who sincerely desires humiliations; who makes them the great object of his prayers; who accepts them with an interior joy, notwithstanding the repugnance of nature; who thanks God for them; who looks upon them as a most precious blessing; who does nothing to be freed from them; who is well pleased that his faults be made known, that he is reproached for his defects, that his virtues be traduced, his reputation sullied; and who, contrary to the will of God, will not allow a single word in his justification,—such a one is truly devoted, and the perfect disciple of Jesus Christ. Now I ask, are there many truly devoted? Are we of the number? Let each one answer to himself—and let him rest assured, that he is as little advanced in devotion as he feels himself remote from this perfection.

CHAPTER XXIII.

MORTIFICATION OF THE SENSES ANOTHER QUALITY OF DEVOTION.

DEVOTION is no less the friend of mortification than of humility; indeed, humility is really the main branch of mortification, its object being to make us die to self-esteem and the love of our own excellence. The other two branches are the death (1) of the inordinate affection which we have for our bodies, and (2) of the natural propensity which leads us to do our own will in all things, and to refer everything to ourselves.

He who is truly devoted spares himself no more in these latter two objects than in the first. He knows that mortification is what God especially demands of him; for prayer is more the work of God than his own. Now all devotion is comprised in the practice of prayer and of mortification. The more progress we make in both, the more devoted we become, and *vice versa.* There is then a division of offices made between God and the soul which is devoted to him; God, ordinarily, takes care of prayer, and the soul takes care of mortification; not that God does not interfere in mortification, or that the soul does not co-operate with him in prayer; but prayer is principally the work of grace, and mortification that of the will.

Mortification of the flesh is indispensable for two principal reasons: first, because the inordinate love of our body, the inclination to sensual pleasures, and the aversion to pain are the source of innumerable sins; and, second, because "the sensual man perceiveth not these things that are of the spirit of God,"* and has no relish for them.

* 1 Cor. ii. 14.

Hence, when a soul gives itself to God, an attraction for exterior mortification is the first thing with which he inspires it. Those who are indifferent or remiss on this point are not truly devoted. In the first fervor one is apt to exceed in this particular, and will go too far, unless restrained by the advice of a prudent director.

What is essential is, never to allow ourselves anything merely with the view of gratifying our senses; never to go in search of any pleasure, even innocent, because it ceases to be innocent the moment we attach ourselves to it and relish it for its own sake; finally, so to regulate that which it is proper to grant to the wants of our body as not to exceed the bounds of what is sufficient. As these bounds have no determined measure, to avoid perplexity and uneasiness on that head, we should earnestly pray God that he himself would direct us, and follow with great docility the lights he will give us. In this point, as well as in all others of a similar nature, God grants the spirit of wisdom and of discretion to all those who ask for it and who are of good will.

From this kind of mortification, which should rather be termed temperance and sobriety, nothing can dispense. But it is not so with regard to austerities. Age, or delicacy of constitution, are just motives for dispensation; great labor of mind or body may supply their place. There are even times in the spiritual life in which God—to deprive the soul of every support—permits hardly any. He who is truly devoted is resolved to do, in this respect, whatever he shall know to be the will of God; and, to avoid mistake, he will take advice. There are whole treatises on this matter, where may be found the details which I here omit.

CHAPTER XXIV.

THAT MORTIFICATION OF THE WILL IS ESSENTIAL TO DEVOTION.

THE mortification of the will is by far more important, more extensive, and, in practice, more difficult than that of the flesh. It knows no bounds nor exceptions; it never should be suspended, and there is no danger of carrying it too far. Were I to expose here all the kinds of death to self through which the will must pass, in order to be absolutely lost in the will of God and to be made one and the self-same thing with his will, it would be the matter of a long treatise. Suffice it to say, that such immolation is different according to God's designs on the soul, and such that an idea can hardly be formed of it until it is personally experienced.

Remember, that to be truly devout is to be devoted to God, and consequently in all things to have no will but his. I say in all things; and God only knows how far this devotedness should extend, since man, by devoting himself, gives back his will, that God may dispose of it according to His own good pleasure. For this purpose, therefore, man must resolve to die to his will, and to second God, in all that He shall do or permit with the view of destroying it.

Do not, however, be alarmed beforehand, nor give reins to your imagination about things that perhaps will never happen. Wait calmly till God manifests his designs. Anticipate nothing, fear nothing, reject nothing, neither offer yourself for anything in particular. Leave all to him. He is infinitely wise; he knows the most secret recesses of your will, and he knows how to bring it round to his own purposes. He will begin with the easiest things, and will gradually lead you to others that will cost you more; and, in this manner, he will lead you, if he thinks proper, to the greatest sacrifices. But he will dispose of all with so much force and sweetness, and will prepare your will in such a way, that it will resist less and less, till at last it will almost lose the power of resistance. All you can give him through your free consent, he will surely incline you to give; and what will not be in your power to give, he will induce you to let him take, in virtue of the absolute offering you have already made of yourself.

Such is the plan which God ordinarily follows. He solicits the soul to give a general and indistinct consent to all that he may be pleased to ordain. This consent once given, he unfolds his particular intentions, either by the events of his providence and the unforeseen circumstances in which he places the soul, or by the temptations and trials to which he exposes it. He proportions his graces and helps to each situation, and the soul has nothing else to do but to yield accordingly to the will of God, as the occasion may require. At first it submits with reluctance and after many struggles, then with promptness, and at last with joy It reaches such a height as no longer to feel interior resistance to anything whatsoever, no longer to desire anything, no longer to fear anything, to have a holy indifference to everything, provided the good pleasure of God be accomplished in its regard. It has then reached the highest degree of conformity, because its will is not only united to God's will, but it is one and the same thing with his.

This is the limit of interior mortification, and at the same time that of devotion. If it do not tend thither, it is no longer devotedness, or it is very imperfect devotedness. Let us humble ourselves and be confounded. Perhaps we fancy ourselves devoted, and we have not as yet a true idea of devotion. "Those who belong to Jesus Christ," says St. Paul, "have crucified their flesh;"* they have fastened it to the cross, after the example of their Master. Is our flesh crucified as that of Christ was,—I do not say during his passion, but throughout the whole course of his life? "Those who belong to him," says the same Apostle, "live not now to themselves, but unto him who died for them, and rose again."† Have we reached this state? Do we labor to attain it? Is Jesus Christ our life? Is his will our will? Do we conceive what it is to live no longer for self, but for Christ?

St. Ignatius on going to his martyrdom said: "I begin to be a disciple of Jesus Christ." The love of his Master was consuming him; he was burning with the

---

* Galat. v. 24.   † 2 Cor. v. 15.

desire of being crushed by the teeth of the wild beasts, yet he dared not say, "I am a disciple of Jesus Christ," but, "I begin to be so; I am only in the first stage;" and what he said he sincerely believed. But we imagine that we do enough, that we even do more than we ought for Jesus Christ; we fancy that we have almost attained perfection! Once more let us humble ourselves. The saints thought very differently of devotion from what we do. They did not flatter themselves that they were devoted; such a title would have shocked their humility; they used to say that they were in constant exercise to become so; they considered themselves as serving an apprenticeship, and this even at the end of their career.

CHAPTER XXV.

VARIOUS QUALITIES OF DEVOTION.

DEVOTION is uniform and invariable. It is a permanent adherence of the heart to God, independent of all the vicissitudes of the spiritual life. It is always the same, in aridity as well as in consolation, in privation as in abundance, in the storm of temptation as in the calm of peace, when abandoned by God as when enriched with the favors of a most intimate union. "Whatever way God deals with me," says the devoted soul, "he is always the same, and deserves at all times faithfully to be served alike." My devotedness should never vary, because he who is its object is immutable.

Devotion is simple and has only one intention. "God alone" is its motto. It studies to purify its motives, raising itself above everything that it may see only God and his will. It has no double look to God and to self; it sees itself only in God and in his good pleasure, which is everything to it.

It is fervent—that is to say, it is always determined to do and to suffer what pleases God, cost what it will. For fervor does not consist in those passing emotions which a sensible grace produces in the soul. Beginners are apt to be deceived by this; at such times they think themselves capable of everything, and they invite God to put them to the test. But let this sensible effect of grace cease, they soon change their notions and their language and they feel all their weakness. True fervor resides in the depths of the will, and it endures as long as the will does not yield to tepidity, to remissness, to sloth; as long as it preserves the same ardor, the same courage, the same activity.

Devotion is faithful, carrying its attention and exactness to an extreme delicacy, yet without scruple or anxiety. It is faithful in little as in great things,—faithful in what is of perfection as in what is of obligation,—faithful to the smallest sign as to the most express commandment. The principle from which it never swerves is, that nothing is little in the service of so great a Master, whose will alone sets a value on things, and that we cannot better testify our love than by anticipating his wishes without waiting for a precise command.

Devotion is discreet, always attentive to guide itself according to the spirit of God; no ways inconsiderate, imprudent, nor excessive; a friend to order, doing everything in the proper time and place, knowing when to be firm or when it should condescend to the weakness of others; exact in its pious practices, or at times relaxing its regularity in behalf of charity.

Devotion does not listen to the imagination, which is the stumbling-block of most pious people, which troubles and disconcerts them; forges for them a thousand vain phantoms, and is always beguiling them to undertake something and then to abandon it; leading them into extravagance, caprice, much levity, and inconstancy. Devotion particularly aims at conquering and despising these freaks. By so doing, it secures great peace of mind, an evenness of temper which nothing disturbs, a serenity of soul which is reflected externally, and shows a placid countenance in the most trying situations.

CHAPTER XXVI.

SOME OTHER QUALITIES OF DEVOTION.

DEVOTION is docile, is not attached to its own ideas, and readily submits them to those who have authority over it, sacrificing to them even that which may seem a conviction and a persuasion; obeying them in spite of the greatest repugnance; adhering to no practice against their will, and making no change in its conduct without their advice.

It does not judge itself either adversely, lest it be discouraged, nor favorably, lest it become presumptuous; equally on its guard against a false humility, which is never satisfied with its progress and finds fault with all its actions, and against a false confidence, which applauds itself for whatever it does and easily presumes on its advancement. It thinks that it is more humble and more safe not to examine itself, nor to pronounce on its state, but to allow those to judge who are charged with its conduct, and to believe them with the same simplicity, whether they approve or condemn.

Severe towards itself, true devotion is indulgent to others; prudently consulting their weaknesses; taking for its own share what is most painful and difficult; and carrying itself at all times a greater burden than it imposes.

It is active without haste, deliberate without slowness, grave without affectation, cheerful without levity. It is not trifling nor scrupulous, nor restless, nor rigid, nor remiss, but keeps in everything the just mean, inclining rather to mercy than to a too exacting justice.

Although zealous for virtue, and always ready to undertake those good works which Providence may throw in its way, it does not go in search of them, but waits. It does not propose, nor intermeddle, nor intrigue; it does not interfere in everything, and take part in everything, as if nothing could be well done unless it direct and assume the charge. It has nothing to do with the affairs of others; it does not inquire about them, nor look curiously upon them, nor pass judgment upon them; it is with the greatest circumspection that it engages in them, when induced by charity, and then it is indefatigable in procuring their success, sparing, for that purpose, neither endeavor nor credit, yet ready at any moment to withdraw, preferring that good deeds of this kind should be done by others than by itself.

Its zeal does not consist in incessantly inveigling bitterly against abuses even the most real. It bewails them before God, and beseeches him to put things in order;

but for itself it bears with them, if it be not charged to correct them; and if it be, it does it with as much meekness and patience as efficacy,—without hurry, precipitancy, or violence. Attentive to its own reformation, it does not set itself up as a reformer. It is too much taken up with its own failings to pay attention to those of others; either it does not see them, or it excuses them ; or, if it cannot excuse them, it is silent, unless it speaks of them through a motive of charity and for the good of the persons interested.

It is a declared enemy of what are called *coteries*, of parties, cabals, and exclusive associations. Not but what it makes choice of some persons with whom it may form a holy intercourse, and with whom it may confidentially converse on holy things; but these unions are the work of grace. There is nothing affected nor mysterious in them, nor anything which shows a contempt of others, as if they were unworthy to be admitted into its society. Much less does it form parties to give popularity to a certain preacher, or to a particular director, and to raise them by depressing others. This party-spirit characterizes false devotion, and true piety holds it in abhorrence.

CHAPTER XXVII.

THAT DEVOTION CORRECTS AND PERFECTS THE CHARACTER.

FROM what has been said, it is evident that one of the great objects of devotion is to reform the character. To this it at first applies us, opening our eyes to our defects, to which we are but too blind,—awakening a desire of overcoming them, a courage to attack them, and a hope of conquering them with the help of grace.

Every one knows that there is no character so perfect that it is not subject to some defect; and that even the best natural qualities are akin to some vice. Meekness degenerates into weakness, into a soft complacence, into indolence. Resolution exposes us to stiffness, harshness, obstinacy. Prudence is often cowardly distrustful, suspicious. Zeal, on the contrary, is bold, presumptuous, rash. It is the same with all other qualities; they are seldom pure, but almost always a mixture of good and bad.

Reason alone will never effect a perfect discrimination. It is not subtle enough to discern the delicate shades which sepaate good and bad qualities, nor just, enough to hit upon the mean between two extremes, nor has it a sufficient command over itself to maintain it with steadiness. Much less can it reconcile two good qualities which seem opposed to each other. This can be only the work of grace, the light of which is infinitely more penetrating and sure, and which, while enlightening the mind, animates and supports the will in an undertaking where there is question of remoulding nature.

When I speak of remoulding nature, it is not to be understood that the character is changed into an opposite one. The foundation of every character is good; why, then, should grace change it? The foundation indeed remains, but whatever self-love has added to it that is vicious disappears, and that which is good is perfected. Each moral quality loses what is in excess and acquires what is wanting to it. They blend together and from their happy union perfect virtue results. Moreover, devotion supernaturalizes the moral qualities and communicates to them something divine which ennobles and sanctifies them.

However, it must be acknowledged that the industry of man, though assisted by grace, seldom brings the work to the highest perfection, and that in the most holy persons there generally remains some defect or excess which flows from the original character, as may be seen in the writings and conduct of a St. Cyprian, a St. Jerome, and of many others.

But when God himself undertakes the work, and when with this view he takes possession of a soul and puts it into the interior life, if this soul be faithful, habitual recollection, prayer, and severe trials radically purify it and pass its character through the crucible till it is without alloy. Such a soul becomes like wax in the hands of the great Artificer, who handles and fashions it as he pleases and makes alterations as profound as they are delicate. In such characters everything seems supernatural; nothing merely human is to be seen; no good quality exceeds or trenches on another, but they are all in perfect harmony. Such were St. Augustin and St. Francis de Sales. How amiable was their devotion! What charity, what uniformity, what admirable evenness of soul in their life and in their conversation, as well as in their writings!

CHAPTER XXVIII.

THAT DEVOTION, FAR FROM CONTRACTING THE MIND, AIDS TO ITS DEVELOPMENT.

DEVOTION is accused of contracting the mind, but those who make this reproach know nothing of devotion. They confine their reflections to the littleness and minutiæ of certain people who affect to be devoted, and they ascribe to devotion the defects of those who conceive it wrongly and practise it badly.

Let us single out any man or woman you wish who regards and practises devotion in the manner I have defined and explained, and see if it has contracted their mind. But what need to do this? Is there necessity for much reflection and argument to convince us that devotion is the only source whence we can draw true, great, and right ideas on the objects the most important to man; which, to the knowledge furnished by pure and sound reason, adds the more solid, surer, and more sublime lights of revelation? Nothing is great but truth; and truth is God; it is whatever emanates from God, whatever tends to God and terminates in him.

How, then, can that mind be contracted which, in matters that are within its reach and that relate to its duties, makes it a rule to consult God and to conform its ideas and judgments to the ideas and judgments of God? Is not God "the Father of lights"? * Is not the eternal Word, "the true light that enlighteneth every man that cometh into this world"? † And some people will have it, that a mind that takes this light

---

* James i. 17.   † John i. 9.

for its rule and guide becomes narrow and little! There is no absurdity, no contradiction equal to this.

It has already been observed that devotion instructs us in what is within our reach, and in what relates to our duties; for it is not necessary that it should go farther. It adapts itself to the capacity of the simple and ignorant, and gives them all that is sufficient for them to conduct themselves as they ought. The truly devout man, whatever be the natural extent of his mind and of his education, has always more reason, more good sense, more penetration and exactness, than if he were not devoted. This is incontestable, and it is all that is necessary to prove what has been asserted. But if a man of great genius, cultivated by an excellent education, give himself to devotion, if in his meditations and studies he preserves a serenity of mind free from prejudice and passion, seeking but the truth, and seeking it only in God,—I maintain that in his researches he will penetrate as far as the bounds of his understanding permit, that he will judge of things the most intricate and the most delicate, as certainly as can be expected from a reason which is not infallible, and that his talents will acquire all the development of which they are susceptible.

St. Augustin was devout. He understood religion and practised it devotedly. Was his mind contracted? Do we know of any mind more extensive, more elevated, and more profound? Would he have had so great, so just, so penetrating views, had he confined himself to the study of eloquence and of profane philosophy? Let us judge from what he himself relates in his "Confessions." Until the age of thirty he applied himself to all kinds of science, and with an indefatigable ardor fought for truth everywhere but in religion! Did he find it?

Did his restless mind find repose? Did he examine truth to the bottom, and develop it as he did afterwards, when he gave himself totally to God and hardly knew any other book besides the Holy Scriptures, and when, to understand them better, he implored the divine assistance by continual prayer?

St. John Chrysostom was devout. Did his devotion do injury to his brilliant genius, or to his great gift of eloquence? Did it not add that nobleness of conception, that exact good sense, that profound philosophy which we admire in his works, and for which he certainly was not indebted to the lessons of Libanius, his master? Would he have been so great a man had he adhered to that sophist, who had designed him for his successor, and had not been torn from him by the Christians, as Libanius complains? Compare the writings of each, and then judge. As much could be said of all the Fathers of the Church, who owe it to devotion that they became the luminaries of their age.

Devotion, therefore, is so far from contracting the mind that, on the contrary, it gives to it all the breadth, all the solidity, all the sagacity of which it is capable. This will appear evident if we consider the nature of the objects proper to devotion, the light which it throws upon other objects, the rules it lays down to judge them, the means it employs, and the obstacles it removes. I except the frivolous arts and acquisitions of mere amusement, which it teaches us to despise, or at least forbids us to give ourselves up to them. This presupposed, is there a single science truly worthy of man, to which devotion, as I have defined it, is not useful, or even necessary, in order to penetrate its true principles, and to trace and to develop its consequences? I leave this to the reflection of my reader. Let him run over philosophy and all its branches,—logic, physics, metaphysics, ethics, political economy, politics, jurisprudence; and then tell me if there be a single one of them which can be possessed and thoroughly discussed without the science of religion, which is their common basis. What is history more than an object of curiosity, and a mere exercise of the memory, if it is separated from Providence, which prepares the events long beforehand, and permits and designs them for wise and worthy ends? And what other mind but one enlightened by solid devotion will be able to view history in the intimate relation which it has always had, and ever will have, to religion? If the great Bossuet had not viewed it in this manner, would his celebrated "Discourse on Universal History" have been so sublime, so eloquent, so instructive? Would it be the masterpiece of the human mind, both in its plan and execution?

If the man truly devoted is to be deemed *narrow-minded* (petit esprit) because he is devoted; because he loves God, and fears to offend Him; because he respects the Church, its ministers, its commandments, and its decisions; because he is exact and conscientious in the management of his affairs, and about the way of making a fortune; because he cultivates piety, virtue, and probity,—I have nothing more to say. I cannot hinder those who have a personal interest in doing so from calling black white, and white black.

CHAPTER XXIX.

THAT DEVOTION ELEVATES THE HEART OF MAN ABOVE ALL THAT IS NOT GOD.

THE same devotion which enlarges and rectifies the mind expands the heart and ennobles the affections. This assertion needs no more proof than the one preceding. That which contracts and debases the heart is self-love, the passions, the esteem and the love of earthly things. Look no farther for the cause of hard-heartedness, of meanness, of injustice, and cruelty, than the egotism which wants all for self, refers all to self, and strives to concentrate all in self. You cannot name me a single vice nor a single defect which does not spring from this root.

Now, what is the aim of devotion, what

its motive? To attack self-love at its foundation, and pursue it to its entire extinction, substituting in its place the love of God, the love of our neighbor, and the well-regulated love of self. Thus devotion re-establishes in man his primitive rectitude, restores order in his affections, forbids every sentiment that proceeds not from God and which tends not to God. It communicates to him a Christian sympathy, which, raising him above himself, extends his benevolence to all mankind; it interests him, by views superior to human nature, in the happiness or misery of his fellow-creatures; it prompts him to relieve them in distress and to rejoice at their prosperity, as if it were his own; it inspires him with a noble disinterestedness, with a modest and compassionate generosity, unknown to that pompous beneficence, which is ever preceded, accompanied, and followed by a glance on self,—in short, it restores to him all the capacity he received from the Creator, and which only can be filled with the divine immensity.

What further aim has devotion? To turn the human passions, which wrangle and contend together to snatch from one another the frivolous and contemptible goods of this world, the enjoyment of which cannot be divided;—to turn them, I say, to their real object, which alone can satisfy them, and which they all may possess in common ; to teach them to love, hate, desire, and fear only what God and right reason require man to love, hate, fear, and desire,—a moral principle which, if faithfully practised, would banish from the world all manner of crimes, and would dry up their very source in the human heart.

What is the final end of devotion? To inspire us with disgust and contempt for earthly things; to point out to us their true end, which is to supply the transitory wants of this mortal life; to convince us that they are made for us, but only for the lowest part of our being, and that our soul is not made for them; to set before the soul solid, eternal, immutable objects worthy of its nature, and proportioned to its desires; to give it a relish for them, to make it ardently long for their possession, and to teach it the surest means of attaining them.

How grand, how noble, how sublime are the sentiments of a man, in whatever condition or state of life, who, through his devotedness to God, is penetrated with these truths! For, in this respect, devotion brings to a level every condition; and the peasant in his hut is greater than the monarch in his palace, if he has the greater piety. Honors and dignities do not puff him up, obscurity and dependence do not degrade him. He is not insolent in prosperity, nor dejected in adversity, nor proud and scornful like the philosopher in mediocrity. If his surroundings raise him above other men, he only sees in them his equals, to whom he owes either assistance or protection. He looks upon himself as inferior to every one who serves God better than he does; and, because there is not one who is not or may not be greater than he before God, he puts himself, in his heart, in the last place. Should he be in an obscure condition, far from envying those who are conspicuous, he rejoices thereat and thanks God for it. Yes, he thanks God for being born in indigence; and if grace spurs him on, he reduces himself to poverty, and even to voluntary beggary. We have seen this in our days; and this grandeur of soul, to him who knows how to prize it, is not one of the least triumphs of devotion. If he has masters, it is God whom he respects, whom he loves, and whom he obeys in them; and there is nothing in serving them that debases him in the sight of God. In a word (for I do not mean to exhaust this subject), he who has really a great heart, which soars above all that is created and knows no superior but God alone, is truly devoted.

CHAPTER XXX.

THE MAN TRULY DEVOUT REGARDS EVERYTHING IN RELATION TO ETERNITY AND TO THE WILL OF GOD.

IT might seem that nothing more is wanting to this portrait of devotion; that even now it greatly surpasses the idea which is generally formed of it. A few more features, however, must be added.

The truly devoted man is one who no longer belongs to time. From the moment that he consecrates himself to God, he is transported, as it were, into the region of eternity; he thinks only on eternity, not with fear, but with joy, as his ultimate destination. He regards everything with reference to eternity, and he has constantly in his thoughts these words of a saint, "What is this to eternity?" What importance is anything to me which passes away with time? I am in this world only as in a place of trial. I am here to serve my apprenticeship in that which I am to do eternally. I am destined to love God, and to be forever happy in the possession of him. This is my end. That uncertain and very small number of days which is allotted me upon earth, is only given me that I may love God through choice, in order to merit as a reward to love him forever. Everything here below should be for me an exercise of love. But love aspires only to give, to sacrifice, to suffer for the object which it loves, to immolate itself at its own good pleasure. This, therefore, is all I have to do; this is the employment of every moment of my life. He whom I love deserves all, and expects all from me. He has loved me with an eternal love, with a love wholly gratuitous and disinterested; with a love to which mine, how ardent soever it may be, can never approach. As the price of his love, he asks for mine; and if he had not been the first to love me, though he had promised me nothing, I should still have a thousand motives for loving him.

The will of God is the only rule of the truly devoted man. In all that happens to him, he sees only that; he attaches himself to that; he blesses it for every thing; he is always contented, provided it be accomplished. He is intimately persuaded that God wills nothing and permits nothing that does not turn to the advantage of those who love him. Whatever comes from his hand—and everything comes from it, except sin—is a blessing to him; and crosses, more than anything else, afford him joy, on account of the resemblance they give to Jesus Christ, the chief and model of souls devoted to God.

Everything helps him to unite himself more and more to him whom he loves; obstacles turn into means. Nothing stops him; he overcomes and breaks down all impediments; he removes every medium that hinders him from joining himself immediately to God, mind to mind, and heart to heart. This holy union is the motive of all his actions and the centre of all his desires. And therefore whatever he loves, he loves it only in God and for God.

Let no one believe, as some falsely imagine, that on account of this his heart is indifferent and insensible. There is no heart more affectionate, more tender, more compassionate, more generous, more grateful, than that of the man truly devoted. His love for his neighbor is modelled after the infinite love of God; indeed, it is but an extension of that which he has for God. Love for his neighbor is a substantial love, a delicate love, an obliging love, which nothing can weaken, and which, on the contrary, is increased by that which seemingly should extinguish it. This, however, does not hinder it being true, in a very just sense, that God is all to the truly devoted man, and that everything else is nothing; because God is his only good and the term of all his affections, which only pass through creatures to fasten themselves on him.

CHAPTER XXXI.

CONDUCT OF THE TRULY DEVOUT MAN IN REGARD TO HIS NEIGHBOR.

But let us look more particularly at the conduct devotion inspires towards our neighbor; for it is upon this point it is most unjustly attacked, and therefore it is necessary to vindicate it from the malignity of its accusers.

I say, then, that since devotion is nothing else but the practice of the purest charity in what regards our neighbor, it has all the characteristics which St. Paul attributes to charity.* Follow me now in the development of these characteristics, applying them to the devoted people with whom we may be acquainted, do justice to those in whom they shine, notwith-

* 1 Cor. xiii. 4-9.

standing the shadows scattered here and there from human frailty.

The man truly devoted, then, is "patient; beareth all things, endureth all things from his neighbor." This endurance is one of the most necessary things in the intercourse of life, and that in which one is most exercised, because the practice of it is continual, and contributes more than anything to the maintenance of domestic peace. It is most needed in the home circle, and with those with whom we habitually live; as the husband and wife with regard to each other, the master with regard to his servants, parents with regard to their children. In general, those who live together, or have frequent intercourse with one another, are constantly exposed to show their natural character such as it is, their whims and a thousand little natural defects. I venture to say that it is easier to be patient on great occasions, when motives of religion sustain us and the fear of offending God puts us on our guard, than to refrain in many trivial circumstances from sallies of ill-humor in words or conduct, which are overlooked or deemed of no consequence. Nevertheless, the want of endurance has sometimes sad consequences. The imagination is enkindled and magnifies the smallest faults; the temper is exasperated; simple repugnance grows into an aversion; we can no longer see nor bear each other; offence is taken at whatever happens; from words we proceed to malicious acts, open animosity, and declared hostility. The matter in the beginning was nothing; it has ended in an incurable hatred. It is just here that the practice of devotion is of great advantage, teaching us to bear with the failings of others as we wish that they should bear with ours.

The devoted man is "full of kindness" —always disposed to oblige. His property, his time, his talents, his credit, belong less to himself than to others. At what moment soever you apply to him, whatsoever you may ask, if it be in his power, he is ready to grant it; he leaves everything, he sacrifices even his exercises of piety, when the interest of his neighbor requires it. He is a stranger to those vain offers, those excuses and evasions which are so common in the world, where, provided that it cost nothing, a great show of good will is set forth, and it is sought to impose on men by the appearance of sincerity. His offers are sincere; he is a slave to his promises; and, when he excuses himself, it is in such manner as to make it felt that it is really painful to him to be unable to grant what is asked.

It is of him alone that it can be said, that "he envieth not;" that he beholds the prosperity of another with as much and more pleasure than his own; that he envies neither the talents nor the success of others, neither the applauses nor the rewards they receive. How should he envy them that which he desires not? He is the first to acknowledge their merit; to praise it, to commend and to set it forth to the best advantage. He is not even jealous of their virtue, of their holiness, or of the graces which God bestows on them, though these are the only treasures he aspires to; indeed, whatever be his desire of loving God, he wishes that others may surpass him in love. How rare a thing is it to be wholly exempt from this base sentiment, yet so natural to man, from which devotion alone can set him free.

The devout man "dealeth not perversely," with levity or with indiscretion: a disposition so important, and of such consequence in society. Much superior is this point to politeness, which only saves the appearances; devotion extends this rule to the judgments and the affections, whence flow all external demonstrations, of which we do not always have control unless we are attentive to what passes within.

Far from being "puffed up" with the temporal or spiritual advantages which he has over others, the truly devoted man disregards them; or, if he thinks of them, he only finds in them motives of humiliation; whereas, he who is not truly devoted is always secretly comparing himself with his neighbor, to give himself the preference and congratulate himself at being "not as the rest of men."* The truly devoted man tries all he can to forget himself, and the judgments which he forms of himself tend only to make him despise himself. This is the most intimate conviction of his heart.

No one is less "ambitious" than he.

---

*Luke xviii. 11.

As much as others are flattered with distinctions and preferments, so much is he averse to them. He thinks so little of elevating himself, of being above others and of commanding, that, on the contrary, he prefers to be abased, to seek the last place, and to obey. He is still more exempt from spiritual ambition, well knowing that it is more dangerous and more odious to God and man. He stifles the smallest germ of it in his heart and never suffers anything to appear exteriorly that might make an impression in his favor.

The devout man "seeketh not his own interest," but is always ready to sacrifice it for the sake of peace and to preserve charity. His great, his only interest, is on account of God to live in peace with all mankind.

He is a stranger to anger, harsh expressions, and to the spirit of contradiction. Meekness accompanies all his words and rules all his proceedings. He chooses rather to yield, when he is in the right, than to maintain his opinion with warmth. Nothing wounds him, nothing offends him, nothing irritates him. One would think that he is insensible, and that he observes nothing, yet his feelings are extremely delicate and nothing out of the way escapes him.

Whilst the man of false devotion is scandalized at everything, and misconstrues everything, "he thinketh no evil," and interprets everything in good part, endeavoring as far as he can to see and represent things in a favorable light, to extenuate real wrongs, and to justify the intention when the action cannot be excused. As he has no malice, he suspects none in others, and, to give credit to an evil report, he must be compelled by evidence.

CHAPTER XXXII.

THE DIFFERENCE BETWEEN THE POLITENESS OF THE WORLD AND THE CORDIALITY OF TRUE DEVOTION.

THE politeness of the world is nothing but dissimulation.* It manifests esteem and friendship only the better to conceal its coolness and contempt,—indifferent to those whom it affects the most to caress, often even wishing evil to those whose interests it seems to espouse the most warmly. The truly devout man "loves without dissimulation;" he shows in his face what he has in his soul; his lips express only what he feels. His characteristic is cordiality—that precious virtue which the world has banished from its commerce to retain but its semblance.

* Rom. xii. 9, etc.

He does not wait till he is prevented by others, but "with honor he prevents them." He forgets the attention that is due to himself, and thinks only of that which charity prompts him to pay to his neighbor. Not that he cannot assert his dignity and maintain the privileges of his station when propriety demands it; but on these occasions he is free from all haughtiness and over-delicate pretension, and on this account his right is the less contested.

Politeness gives only that it may receive; it makes advances on one occasion only that they may be returned to it on another. It measures and graduates its civilities, and exacts at least as much attention as it bestows, and is always apprehensive of being slighted or undervalued. It is not so with devotion. Without derogating from what belongs to place and condition, it knows how to be affable, gracious, obliging; it banishes constraint from social intercourse and it puts itself on a level with those with whom it converses; its advances are frank, natural, disinterested, without any thought of return.

Human compassion has often but bare words, or, at most, barren sentiments. It is partial, inconstant, and, after the first effusion, is soon spent. Sometimes the evils it beholds by their very excess inspire it with more horror than pity, and if it relieve them, it is only with an uprising of the heart and averted look. It but too frequently happens that the humanity on which it prides itself is affected and blended with ostentation; that it does good only for the sake of show, and, while revealing the hidden misery of others, causes them to repent of giving their confidence.

Devotion does not fall into any of these faults. Its commiseration extends to all the unfortunate: "communicating," from the heart, in their evils and in their "necessities," as if they were its own. It relieves them effectually by taking not only from its superfluity, but even from its necessity. No sort of misery disgusts it; and the greater the misery is, the more eager it is to succor it. It accompanies its charities with an air of interest, of sensibility, of tenderness that moves, consoles, and gladdens the afflicted. Particularly attentive to degraded indigence, it discovers it and spares it the confusion of an explanation; it often conceals the hand that gives assistance, or does it so secretly that no one ever surmises it or hears a whisper of it.

Charity often gives to the man truly devout the interior dispositions of his neighbor. "He rejoices with them that rejoice and weeps with them that weep."* His soul enters into the sentiments of

* Rom. xii. 15.

those who approach him, and is affected with all which touches them. This is not flattery nor mere politeness; it is the true and profound interest of a brother, who shares the good and the evil of his brethren and considers them as his own.

Lastly, if we consider, on the one hand, how far humanity, education, and politeness contribute to the utility, security, comfort, and enjoyment of social life, and, on the other, the happiness which results from devotion well understood and practised, and what would further result were it more generally diffused,—we shall be forced to acknowledge that all the advantage is on the side of devotion, and that there is no comparison between them. To the devout man belongs the encomium bestowed in Scripture on Moses, "of being beloved of God and men;"* because he serves God in God, and does to man all

---

* Ecclus. xlv. 1.

the good he can. If he be not at all times loved by men, it is because they are wicked, envious, and ungrateful; because they despise virtue, and refuse to do it justice.

CHAPTER XXXIII.

THE MAN TRULY DEVOUT POSSESSES ALL CIVIL QUALITIES.

IF the devoted man is what he ought to be, he is a good husband, a good father, a good master, a good friend, a good citizen, a good subject; because the essence of devotion consists in a faithful discharge of all the duties which are annexed to these several spheres, and to others of a similar nature. There is no case in which it authorizes a neglect of the least of the natural or civil obligations of society, or in which it does not severely condemn those who fail in such obligations. This is not all; devotion alone displays to us the full extent of these duties, it binds us in conscience to study them, and makes us take interest and pleasure in fulfilling them, at all times and in every circumstance.

All things else being equal, compare in each state, in each profession, the devout man with him who is not so. See which is the more learned, the more assiduous, the more honest, the more exact, the more delicate, and the more disinterested; which it is who succeeds the better, of whom the public complains the less, and with whom it is more pleased. Glance over the most elevated stations; examine by whom they have been the better filled,—by the friends or by the enemies of devotion. One may be devout and want talents,—but he neither wants zeal, nor probity, nor love for the right. The faults occasioned through want of genius should not be imputed to devotion, since it never prompts us to engage in a charge, an office, a profession for which we are not fitted; since it requires us to omit nothing that may fit us for them; and even to resign them and lay them down, if the public and individuals suffer by our retaining them. It is never from devotion that frauds, misdemeanors, injustices, violence, and the abuse of authority proceed, no more than negligence, the want of application, and all the other consequences of a culpable ignorance. All good is to be set down to its account; to all evil it is a stranger, and to make it responsible for anything of the kind is the height of injustice. This is, in general, what a real devout man is in his relations to his fellow-man and to society.

CHAPTER XXXIV.

THE TRULY DEVOUT MAN POSSESSES THE ONLY TRUE HAPPINESS THAT CAN BE ENJOYED ON EARTH.

So far as what personally regards the devout man, devotion procures him the only true happiness to be enjoyed upon earth. It never has happened that one truly devout had reason to repent his being so, and it never will happen. It will be said that he hates and despises himself, combats and renounces himself. I grant it; and it is precisely in this that he finds peace, equanimity of soul, and joy. It is certain, both from reason and the principles of faith, and demonstrated by constant and universal experience, that the good things of this world, riches, honors, and pleasures, cannot satisfy the soul, but only provoke its hunger, without appeasing it; that the passions are the principal source of the misfortunes which oppress mankind; and that, for the inevitable evils of this life, no other philosophy than that of religion can help us to bear them, or teach us the proper use of them.

It is also certain and demonstrated by experience that, God being man's only good, devotion which brings him to God —which tends to unite him to God—is the true and the only principle of his happiness; that it preserves him from sin, which is his sovereign evil; that it secures him from the misfortunes which are the fruit of his own passions; that in regard to the other evils, whether natural or occasioned by the injustice and the malice of man, it teaches him to overcome them with patience, and to draw from them wonderful advantages; while in regard to temptations, trials, and other spiritual sufferings, it persuades him that they are not evils, but real blessings; that they are remedies which expiate sin, or preserve him from it,—occasions to practise virtue, as well as means to sanctify him and to dispose him to divine union. Thus it lifts him above all human accidents, above the vicissitudes of the spiritual life, even above himself, and establishes him in an unalterable peace.

On the other hand, God, who is rich in mercy and who never suffers himself to be outdone in generosity, devotes himself, if I may be allowed to say so, to the man who is devoted to him; he treats him as his child, he takes care of him as "the apple of his eye" (it is the expression which he himself makes use of);* he lavishes upon him his aid, his consolations, his favors; in short, he is eager to convince him, by the strongest and most

* Zach. ii. 8.

assured proofs, that he gains all in sacrificing all to him, and that the highest happiness of the creature is only to be found in the privation of everything else, and even of itself, in order to secure the possession of the infinite good.

Let not the reader accuse me of falsehood or exaggeration. On the contrary, let him be assured that all that has been said falls far short of the reality. We have on this subject the unanimous testimony of the saints; I refer you to them. You have their writings; consult them, and see if they say less than I do. There is not one amongst them who has not borne witness that he was happy in God's service, that he had never been happy before, and that it is the only way of being happy. Should you say that you have not experienced this happiness, although you have served God for many years, that must proceed from your not serving him with the same devotedness as the saints;

from your blending, with your devotion, much negligence, much laxity, and much reserve; from your seeking yourself instead of seeking God, and from your self-love, which tyrannizes over your soul by fear, by desire, by vain regrets, and idle forebodings, by murmurs, interior rebellions, and by the resistance it opposes to the reign of the love of God.

CHAPTER XXXV.

THAT JESUS CHRIST IS THE GRAND MODEL OF PERFECT DEVOTEDNESS.

IF the reader ask for a model of perfect devotion, what other can be proposed than that which has been given to us all in the person of Jesus Christ? Listen to this Divine Master, and study his conduct. He came upon earth only to teach us in what true devotion consists. All the lessons of his heavenly doctrine are reducible to that of devotedness. His whole life was nothing else but the most absolute devotedness practised in the most excellent manner.

The moment he came into the world he devoted himself to God his Father as a victim to repair the outrages done to his glory, and to effect the reconciliation of man. From that instant the great cross which he was to carry was offered to him; that cross comprised the whole course of his life, and was to become every day harder and heavier from the manger to his last gasp. It united to an incomprehensible degree every kind of suffering and opprobrium which could be borne by a soul sustained by all the power of the divinity. It was to exhaust on him the scourge of divine justice. It was to equal and surpass all the pains due to man's enormous and innumerable iniquities. His soul, infinitely illuminated with the divine light, measured the extent of this cross, distinctly knew all its rigors, foresaw and felt beforehand its unutterable torments.

He accepted it with all the submission, all the love, all the generosity that a God-Man was capable of. It was always present to his thoughts; it was always dear to his heart. He continually hastened by his desires the consummation of his sacrifice; and the extreme vehemence of these desires was perhaps the greatest of his torments. For, how great soever the excess of it may have been, his love went incomparably beyond, and made him wish to suffer still more, if it could be, for the glory of his Father and for our salvation.

This is the sublime, the divine model of devotedness: this the most faithful and the only true expression of that which God deserves on our part, and of the service we owe to him. It is only in view of this wonderful devotedness that God is pleased to be satisfied with ours, weak, imperfect, and unworthy as it is of his sovereign majesty. Our devotedness, how far soever it may reach, how great soever it may be conceived to be, is of no value in itself. It is insufficient to expiate the smallest of our offences and to merit for us the least degree of glory. There never was but one devotedness in itself pleasing to God,—that of Jesus Christ. He accepts only that; he regards only that, and from it ours derives all its value.

Let us, therefore, cast our eyes upon this perfect and unique Model, and let us, at the very beginning, imprint deeply in our minds this grand truth, that God is so much above us, or, to speak more properly, that God is so much all, and we so much nothing, that it is impossible for us, by the highest and most generous devotedness that can be imagined, I do not say to attain to what he has a right to expect from us, but even to do anything that may draw down upon us his least regard, or may render us worthy of the slightest mark of his benevolence.

After this, having profoundly humbled and annihilated ourselves, let us entreat him to inspire us himself with an act of devotedness that he will deign to accept, and implore him to make us produce this act with all the love that can enter into the human heart, and to support us by the power of his grace in the faithful and constant accomplishment of all the sacrifices which such an act implies.

Finally, because we are nothing of ourselves, and prone to sin from the perversity of our will, because there is nothing that is good in us which is not a gift of God,—let us unite our devotedness to that of Jesus Christ, conjuring this divine Saviour to communicate to it some share of the merits of his devotedness, to offer it to his Father with his own, and to prevail on him, through his all-powerful mediation, graciously to accept it.

CHAPTER XXXVI.

THREE EFFICACIOUS MEANS TO ACQUIRE TRUE DEVOTION.

DOUBTLESS the essential point is rightly to apprehend the act of devotedness, and to form it in the heart with a full and entire will; for all depends upon knowing the nature and the qualities of our engagement with God, and on generously embracing all its obligations. We may well say here that the beginning is half of the whole.

But it is only the half; we must come to the practice. Perhaps you will wish to know by what means. I will not answer this question in full here. It will be the subject of another book to follow this, under the title of "Spiritual Maxims," in which I hope to say enough to put beginners on the way. I will, however, propose here three general means which will lead those who observe them very far.

In the first place, the fact of our being devoted should be constantly present to our mind, according to the example of Jesus Christ. The moment when we devote ourselves, whether in prayer or at communion, is a moment of fervor and of a strong and sensible grace. Then the soul is, as it were, lifted above itself and transported to God. But this moment soon passes; the fervor declines; the sensible impression of grace vanishes. The soul comes back to itself and returns to its former state. A thousand unavoidable cares which distract it will cause it to lose sight of the engagement which it has contracted, if it be not careful to recall it often, and to render the recollection habitual. This recollection rouses and supports it, animates its languor and excites its courage, and is at once a curb to check it and a spur to urge it on.

The second means consists in conforming ourselves in all respects to the example of Jesus Christ, as persons devoted to God—that is to say, to no longer dispose of our ourselves, to no longer form views and projects of any kind whatever, but to leave ourselves in the hands of God, and to undertake nothing but by the inspiration of his grace; for, indeed, he never fails to manifest his will to a soul determined to accomplish it. We must admit neither fear nor desire concerning any other objects than those which belong to our devotedness; but we must ever fear whatever may make us swerve from it, ardently desiring to be faithful. We must consider ourselves henceforward as being under the special guidance of Providence, and leave the care of our interior to God without solicitude, without too much reflection on our state, without curiously inquiring into the reasons of what happens to us. We must accept with equal thankfulness what comforts us and what afflicts us, what troubles us and what composes us, what contradicts us and what gratifies us, what depresses us and what lifts us up. We must believe without hesitation that God has in view only our welfare, and that, provided we adhere to his will, things in appearance the most adverse will turn out to our advantage.

Thus to exercise ourselves in submitting to every event, whether temporal or spiritual, is not the work of one day, but the business of our whole life. We must be a long while apprentices in this science before we become masters; and then we only become skilful after repeated faults by which we are humiliated and corrected. But it is indispensable to enter from the beginning into this general disposition, without which there is no practice of devotedness.

The third means is to have Jesus Christ always before our eyes in order to copy him, and express him in our interior and exterior conduct. We must entreat him to form in us his own image, and to hold us under his hand, like an immovable and well-stretched canvas, ready to receive all the traits of this adorable original. For it is Christ himself who works upon our souls and sketches his own portrait, to which he afterwards adds colors and the finest strokes of the pencil when we put no obstacle in his way.

As God made the material world by his Son, it is also by him that he makes the spiritual and supernatural world; and this world only becomes what it ought to be by its resemblance to Jesus Christ. The saints of the Old Testament were figures of him, and those of the New Testament have no other model; and when all the traits of the God-Man shall have been imprinted upon the elect, according to the designs of the eternal Father, the universe will come to an end. "For," says St. Paul, "whom God foreknew, he also predestinated to be made conformable to the image of his Son."*

* Rom. viii. 29.

CHAPTER XXXVII.

REFLECTIONS ON THE CHARACTERISTICS OF TRUE DEVOTION.

IF devotedness to God, after the example of Jesus Christ, be the first duty of every one who bears the name of Christian, with much greater reason is it the duty of those whose office it is to preach it to others, to teach them its practice, and to set them the example of it. None the less is it the duty of those whom God has withdrawn from the troubles of life, that they may devote themselves to his service in a more special manner. And yet, are there many truly devoted in the sacerdotal or in the religious state? I say it with sorrow—they are almost as few in number as the gleanings after the reapers and the grapes after the vintage.

What, then, is the good soil in which this seed being sown will fructify? God knows it, and it is for that soil he has led me to write. These souls will relish, will understand, will practice devotion.

As to others, I already hear them exclaim and complain that I carry things too far; that I demand too much, and that there is no possibility of being devout in the manner which I point out. But is it I who will have it so? Is it not the very nature of the matter? Reason as much as you please on devotion, modify it, temper and soften it as much as you can, you never will be able to harmonize grace and nature, God and the world, the love of God and self-love; and as long as this union will be impossible, so long shall I be in the right, and so long shall I have demanded nothing but what is just and even necessary.

I have pushed things too far! In what? In styling devotion devotedness or a consecration? But it is the meaning of the word. Is it in adhering to the idea of devotedness? On what other idea was my whole book to rest? Am I wrong in asserting that the devotedness which has God for its object should be interior, without reserve and division; that it should proceed from love, that it should inspire confidence, that it should dispose us to abandon ourselves to God; that it should be humble, mortified, and the like, as may be remembered? Have I said too much? Have I even said all that could be said on each of these characteristics? And if by a culpable caution I had lessened the truth, would not those who accuse me of going to extremes have been the first to charge me with remissness?

Would I have said less if I had given for title to this work, "The Characteristics of True Charity"? and if, in unfolding the two grand precepts of the love of God and the love of our neighbor, on which hang the law and the prophets, I had applied to them all that I have ascribed to devotion?

Would I have said less if, speaking to the disciples of Jesus Christ, and addressing to them the very words of their Master, I had interpreted to them his lessons and his doctrine according to the sense of the Apostles and the Fathers of the Church? or if, in proposing to them Christ as a model, I had strongly represented to them the indispensable necessity of imitating his interior dispositions towards God, his Father, and towards man, and the virtues which shone throughout his whole life from the manger to the cross?

Would I have said less if I had placed before them the example of the primitive Christians, our fathers in the faith, and had asked them if, having the same duties and the same obligations, they were not bound to have the same sentiments, the same conduct, and the same devotion? Let it not be said that the circumstances are not the same. I could easily prove that the present circumstances are more delicate and more dangerous to salvation.

I conclude that I could not have said less without betraying the cause of my great Master, and that we cannot do less without injuring the dearest interests of our soul. The glory of God, for which we are created, the eternal happiness to which we are called, as well as our present happiness, are concerned. The matter well deserves mature deliberation, and a prudent decision.

FINIS.

www.ingramcontent.com/pod-product-compliance
Lightning Source LLC
Chambersburg PA
CBHW020926230426
43666CB00008B/1591